The Regulation
of the
Security Markets

By

Willard E. Atkins
George W. Edwards
Harold G. Moulton

THE BROOKINGS INSTITUTION
WASHINGTON, D. C.
1946

THE BROOKINGS INSTITUTION

The Brookings Institution—Devoted to Public Service through Research and Training in the Social Sciences—was incorporated on December 8, 1927. Broadly stated, the Institution has two primary purposes: the first is to aid constructively in the development of sound national policies; and the second is to offer training of a supergraduate character to students of the social sciences.

The responsibility for the final determination of the Institution's policies and its program of work for the administration of its endowment is vested in a self-perpetuating board of trustees. It is the function of the trustees to make possible the conduct of scientific research under the most favorable conditions, and to safeguard the independence of the research staff in the pursuit of their studies and in the publication of the results of such studies. It is not a part of their function to determine, control, or influence the conduct of particular investigations or the conclusions reached, but only to approve the principal fields of investigation to which the available funds are to be allocated, and to satisfy themselves with reference to the intellectual competence and scientific integrity of the staff. Major responsibility for "formulating general policies and co-ordinating the activities of the Institution" is vested in the president. The by-laws provide also that "there shall be an advisory council selected by the president from among the scientific staff of the Institution."

PREFACE

This book is the ninth in an integrated series of studies pertaining to postwar readjustment and reconstruction. The preceding publications carry the following titles:

The present study seeks to clarify the basic issues involved in the regulation of the security markets. It analyzes the forces and conditions responsible for federal regulation, summarizes in nontechnical form the major purposes and provisions of the eight acts pertaining to the security business which have been passed since 1933, and then concentrates on the practical issues arising out of the administration of these laws.

The study also reveals the underlying causes of the security market stagnation of the thirties and explains why an extensive expansion of security flotations will inevitably occur in the postwar period.

The study was prepared jointly by the undersigned and Professor Willard E. Atkins of New York University and Professor George W. Edwards of the College of the City of New York. The co-operating committee of the Institution consisted of Cleona Lewis and Karl T. Schlotterbeck.

Harold G. Moulton,
President.

May, 1946

The study upon which this book is based was made possible by funds granted by The Maurice and Laura Falk Foundation of Pittsburgh. However, the Falk Foundation is not the author, publisher, or proprietor of this publication and is not to be understood as approving or disapproving by virtue of its grant any of the statements or views expressed herein.

CONTENTS

CHAPTER I

POSTWAR CAPITAL REQUIREMENTS

The organization, the development, and the day-to-day operations of business enterprises require the use of capital funds. Such funds are needed to acquire or construct plant and equipment, to finance the processes of production, and to carry sales made on a credit basis instead of for cash.

The capital funds required by business are commonly classified as either fixed capital or working capital. Fixed capital funds are those expended for land, buildings, and equipment. Working capital funds are those used to pay for such items as raw materials and supplies and to provide pay-roll money.

The term "capital," it should be observed, has been used in the preceding paragraph to relate to *funds* needed by business rather than to concrete physical properties such as industrial buildings, machines, tools, and inventories of raw materials and supplies. Capital will be used in this sense throughout the book, for we are here concerned with the raising of money in the financial markets with which to operate the business enterprise system.

Capital funds for the initiation, operation, and expansion of business enterprises may be secured in a number of ways: (1) from the savings of individual owners, partners, or original shareholders; (2) from earnings of the going enterprise; (3) from loans; and (4) from the sale of securities to individual and institutional investors.

1

In the past, funds for starting a business were usually contributed by individual owners or partners. Today, under the corporate form of organization, the initial capital is usually provided by a small group of organizers and perhaps a limited number of friends and acquaintances who can be induced to assume the risks which seem to be involved. Although cases to the contrary can be cited, particularly in the public utility field, securing funds from the general public usually must wait until an enterprise gets on its feet and displays some tangible evidence of ability to make profits. Additional capital may then be secured through a public offering of bonds or shares.

Once a business gets started, part of the funds used for capital expansion are derived from internal sources—by plowing back earnings. In the case of individual proprietors and partnerships, this commonly meant—under the so-called "New England" practice—the limiting of withdrawals to essential living expenses in order to conserve funds for the expansion of the business.[1] In the case of the modern corporation, the management simply decides not to disburse the full earnings in dividends. The undis-

---

[1] Karl Marx comments on behalf of the early capitalists. ". . . On the other hand, the average profits were low, and to accumulate extreme parsimony was requisite. They lived like misers, and were far from consuming even the interest on their capital. . . . Even in the early part of the 18th century, a Manchester manufacturer, who placed a pint of foreign wine before his guests, exposed himself to the remarks and headshakings of all his neighbors. Before the rise of machinery, a manufacturer's evening expenditure at the public-house where they all met, never exceeded sixpence for a glass of punch, and a penny for a screw of tobacco. . . ." Vol. I, *The Process of Capitalist Production,* translated from the Third German Edition by Samuel Moore and Edward Aveling. Frederick Engels, ed. (1921), pp. 651-52.

tributed earnings are usually carried in due course to the earned surplus account.

Another method of raising capital within the business is by the accumulation of hidden reserves through such practices as charging *excessive* depreciation on plant and equipment. This results in showing smaller profits than are actually being currently earned and employed by business. *True* depreciation is not intended to provide funds for capital expansion, but only for the eventual replacement of existing plant and equipment. It should be noted, however, that if the new plant can be purchased at less cost than the original, the replacement funds may provide for some expansion; and contrariwise that if costs of construction have risen, the funds accumulated may not be adequate to replace the existing properties.

The larger part of the capital funds required for expansion has been obtained, however, from external sources. These funds were raised in what is known as the general investment market. The process of bringing together the corporation seeking funds and individuals having excess funds involves the services of a number of intermediary financial institutions. The types of institutions and some of the relationships involved are illustrated in the diagram on page 16.

The trends of the thirties led many to conclude that future capital needs would be relatively small.

The low level of security financing and bank borrowing during the thirties was commonly referred to as "the stagnation of the capital markets." It was observed that corporations seemed to have become largely independent of external sources of funds, that provision for the replacement of plant and equipment, and for such little expansion as was necessary, came largely from internal sources—that is, from depreciation reserves and corporate savings.

During this period the investment banking business was at a low ebb and confined largely to refunding operations. There was a great reduction both in the capital and in the personnel employed, and grave fears were expressed with respect to the future of this once flourishing field of enterprise. The commercial banking business was similarly compressed. Outstanding commercial loans showed an almost continuous decline, and the earnings of the banks became increasingly dependent upon acquisition of federal government securities.

The interpretation placed upon these trends by the Temporary National Economic Committee and numerous others was that the stagnation in the capital markets had become a more or less permanent feature of the national economy. It was emphasized that the private enterprise system had spent its driving force, that the economy had reached the stage of maturity. Consequently, the expansion of private capital in the future would proceed at a very slow rate. Moreover, it was held that the bulk of such expansion as might occur could readily be financed out of internal business savings. Thus it appeared that the need for extensive flotations of new issues in the general capital market would steadily diminish.

In the postwar period two factors combine to increase enormously the demand for capital funds.

The first of these factors is the expected increase in volume of business activity as compared with that of the late thirties. Emphasis is being placed upon the paramount necessity of maintaining a high level of employment. Moreover, thanks to the accumulated deficiencies of consumer goods and the abundance of available purchasing power, there appears good reason for believing that we shall have, at least for some time, a level of employment and production very much higher than that of prewar years.

. The number of jobs necessary for satisfactory employment conditions is usually estimated at from 55 to 57 millions as of 1947, of which something like 2 millions will be in the armed services. If this goal is realized, the level of employment in private enterprise would be over 20 per cent above that of the year 1940 and from 8 to 10 per cent above the level of 1944, when about 51 millions were employed in civilian activities.

Such an increase in employment and production will necessitate a very great increase in the volume of capital funds, as compared with 1940: (1) Operation of existing plant and equipment at full capacity will require a substantial increase in operating money. (2) Large capital outlays will be involved in some industries in connection with reconversion and in most industries in connection with physical rehabilitation. (3) A considerable expansion of plant and equipment—in new as well as in old industries— will be called for. (4) Given a fair prospect for international economic and political stability, and a recognition of the underlying requirements for sound credit relations, foreign loans and investments may be resumed on a considerable scale. The financial requirements involved in this expansion program will give us, if successful, a capital market situation bearing little resemblance to that prevailing throughout the thirties.

The second general factor calling for an increase in the demand for capital funds after the war is the higher level of commodity prices that is likely to prevail, as compared with the prewar period. A higher level of prices means higher costs for rehabilitation, higher costs for replacement of worn-out or obsolete machinery, higher costs for new construction of plant and equipment, higher costs of raw and semi-finished materials, higher costs of finished inventories, and higher costs of labor.

The view that wholesale prices in the early postwar years are likely to be much higher than in the late thirties—perhaps from 40 to 60 per cent higher —finds support in the impracticability of reducing wage rates. Labor not only opposes reductions in wages, but insists that there must be sharp increases to compensate for the loss of overtime war pay. The administration is sympathetic to this argument and is giving support to labor in its aspirations for higher wage rates. While an effort is being made to restrain price advances, it is generally recognized that at the least a gradual upward spiral is under way.

Wages, together with salaries, constitute much the largest item of business costs. In addition to the direct labor costs in the manufacture of finished products, there are the indirect labor costs reflected in the prices of the raw materials which must be purchased and in the costs of transportation, power, and fuel.

A high level of wage rates will inevitably carry with it a high level of prices for farm products, both foodstuffs and raw materials. Under existing law we are committed to the maintenance of farm prices at not less than 90 per cent of parity for two full calendar years after the *official* end of the war; and, as a matter of policy, full parity appears likely to be the goal. It should be borne in mind that if industrial prices rise, agricultural parity prices will have to be adjusted upward in order to preserve their relative position. Accordingly, the costs of the agricultural raw materials used by industry will doubtless continue to be very much higher than before the war.

The conclusion that prices are likely to continue to rise, it will be observed, is not based upon a conception of runaway inflation resulting from fiscal and monetary policies or from superabundant purchasing power carried over from wartime accumulations. It is based upon cost considerations alone.

The influence of the price level on the demand for capital funds has been almost entirely overlooked.

Discussions of capital requirements have ordinarily proceeded on the assumption that the primary, if not the only, factor in the demand for capital funds is the volume of production. This is because, in considering capital, economists have been almost entirely concerned with physical capital—plant and equipment and other so-called capital goods. From the point of view of the financial requirements of business, however, the level of prices and money costs is a separate factor which may be quite as important as the physical volume of output. It requires only a moment's reflection to see that if wage rates and raw material prices should rise, say 50 per cent, the amount of pay-roll money and dollar inventories would have to be increased in roughly the same proportions. New plant and equipment, and replacements of existing plant and equipment, would also require increased fixed capital investment.

The importance of the rising price level factor may be illustrated by reference to the period of World War I. Between 1913 and 1920 the level of wholesale prices rose approximately 120 per cent. In comparison, the expansion in the physical volume of production was very small. Under these circumstances the increase in the volume of capital funds required was out of all proportion to the actual expansion of production.

The chart on the following page shows the changes which occurred between 1913 and 1921 inclusive in: (1) the level of wholesale prices; (2) the volume of industrial production; and (3) the amount of commerical bank loans outstanding. While the comparisons are far from precise, the general trend is nevertheless clearly indicated.

The volume of security flotations was not large during the war period because, in the interests of government financing, the private capital market was virtually closed. In fact, there was an actual decline during the war period because of the restrictions imposed. In consequence, the additional funds required had to be obtained almost entirely from the commercial banks; hence the expanding financial requirements are directly reflected in the increasing volume of bank loans outstanding. The total increased from approximately 15 billions in 1913-14 to 22.5 billions in 1918, and to approximately 31 billions in 1920 when the peak of prices was reached.

RISING PRICES AND INCREASING CAPITAL REQUIREMENTS, 1913-21[a]
(1913 = 100)

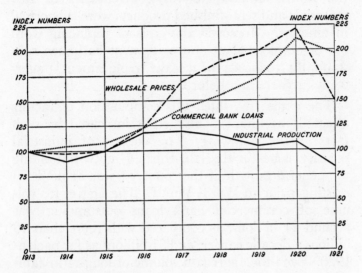

[a] Data from official sources.

The stagnant situation in the late thirties reflects conditions almost exactly the opposite of those prevailing during World War I. First, the physical volume of production, except for a brief interval in 1937, remained at levels below those of a decade earlier. Second, flotations of new issues for expansion purposes were of negligible proportions—because of unutilized existing facilities and uncertainties with respect to the future. Third, the level of prices and of costs was substantially below that of the preceding decade.

Wholesale prices had fallen between the late twenties and the late thirties as much as 20 per cent. Though wage rates had risen meanwhile, the effect had been offset by rapid increases in productive efficiency. Because of the lower level of costs, the funds required to carry inventories of raw materials and semi-finished products were subnormal in amount. Moreover, the costs of replacing worn out or obsolete plant and equipment had been substantially reduced; hence the replacement money went further than before.

The extent to which this combination of factors affected the financial markets is indicated by such facts as the following: The volume of industrial security issues in the late thirties—notwithstanding the general growth of the country—was at the level existing prior to World War I. The aggregate volume of commercial bank loans outstanding was around 21 billions, as compared with more than 40 billions a decade earlier, and 31 billions as far back as 1920. Even the aggregate volume of long-term capital, as measured by bonds, stocks, surplus, and undivided profits, had decreased materially as compared with the late twenties.[2]

*Why was there no important increase in
private capital financing during World War II?*

From 1940 to 1945 we had an unprecedented expansion in industrial output and also a substantial rise in the general level of prices. According to the foregoing analysis, it would seem that these developments should have called for a very great expansion of private security flotations and commercial bank borrowings during the war years. But during most of this period new issues remained at the depressed levels of the late thirties, and there was only a small

[2] Based upon U. S. Treasury *Statistics of Income* covering all nonfinancial corporations.

increase in the volume of commercial bank loans outstanding. This sharp contrast with developments in World War I requires explanation.

During the first world war, as we have seen, business enterprisers obtained the bulk of the funds required from commercial bank loans. During the second world war a large part of the necessary funds was obtained from the government. The government provided fixed capital for war production purposes in two principal ways: the first was by the construction of plants, operated either by government or by private companies; the second was by loans to private enterprises with which to expand plant facilities and especially equipment. Working capital funds were furnished by the government in a variety of ways. These included such methods as: supplying inventories under *cost plus fixed fee* contracts; advance payments on contracts, and progress payments; and extending loans to business enterprises through the Reconstruction Finance Corporation, the Smaller War Plants Corporation, and the Federal Reserve Banks. In addition, accumulated federal income and excess profits tax reserves, and renegotiation reserves, temporarily provided large funds for current use.[3]

These methods of financing found reflection in increasing government deficits and in the expansion in bank holdings of government bonds. In the nature of the case they were not reflected in private security flotations or commercial bank loans to business.[4]

[3] For an illuminating discussion of these methods of financing, see Charles C. Abbott, *The Financial Situation of Industry After Two Years of War,* (1943).

[4] To be sure, a considerable volume of direct financing by banks occurred in the form of the so-called V-Loans.

*How the turning off of the government financial
spigot will affect private financial markets.*

The elimination of war demands and the disappearance of the methods of financing employed during the war will of course necessitate extensive readjustments. Immediately speaking, the aggregate volume of operating money required by business as a whole will decline somewhat because of the shrinkage in the volume of national production and hence in pay roll and other disbursements. However, two factors will operate to increase the amount of working capital for a given volume of business. The first is the disappearance of government contracts—involving furnishing inventories, making advance and progress payments, and prompt settlements, and their replacement by private sales involving no such contributions, much slower payments, and greater risks. Second, when sales were made to the government, no credit extensions were involved; but, with the return to sales through private channels, extensive manufacturing, wholesale, retail, and consumer credits will be required.

Four years of profitable operations have enabled many businesses to improve their financial position by conserving a portion of their earnings. A scrutiny of the balance sheets of a large number of corporations reveals, however, that the situation varies widely in the different lines of industry, and also as between corporations in the same line. Moreover, the adequacy of funds for early postwar operations is affected by costs of reconversion and the delays incident to the resumption of peacetime business. Here also the situation varies markedly in different industries. No generalization applicable to all industry is possible.

In any case, it is clear that we shall have a very great increase in liquid capital requirements as compared with prewar years. If, as appears probable, the volume of production is some 25 per cent above that of 1940 and the level of costs and prices is 40 to 60 per cent higher, the conclusion cannot be escaped that the requirements for capital funds in the early postwar years will be vastly greater than those of the stagnation period of the thirties.

Looking forward over the next three years, three factors will make for still further expansion in capital requirements. First, we are now in the midst of still further advances in wage and other costs which will necessitate larger supplies of funds for pay roll and other working capital purposes. Second, an unusual volume of replacements of worn-out and obsolete plant and equipment is necessary—all of which will have to be constructed on the new high-cost basis. Depreciation reserves that seemed adequate on the low-cost basis of the thirties are not now likely to prove sufficient for the needs.[5] Third, a vast expansion program is indispensable to further economic progress and higher standards of living. This expansion, whether in housing, in transportation, or in manufacturing, will have to be carried out on a very much higher cost basis than that which prevailed before the war.

[5] This problem is thoroughly discussed in a recent publication of the Brookings Institution entitled *Depreciation Policy and Postwar Expansion,* by Lewis H. Kimmel.

CHAPTER II

AN OVER-ALL VIEW OF THE CAPITAL MARKET

Over the past century or so, numerous types of financial enterprises have been developed, which together constitute the mechanism of the money market. These agencies include commercial banks, investment banks, savings banks, insurance companies, corporate trustees, investment companies, security exchanges, etc. Through the activities of these institutions, the savings of individuals are made available to corporations for fixed and working capital purposes. Thus, those who supply investment money are in effect brought into contact with those who demand funds for purposes of production and expansion.

The mechanism of the money market and the flow of funds from ultimate savers to operating corporations is graphically shown on page 16. The arrows indicate the direction of the flow of funds. Moving in the opposite direction are pieces of paper —in the form of securities, promissory notes, etc.— which evidence the transaction.

The *working* capital section of the diagram is connected with both commercial banking and investment banking institutions. A part of a corporation's working capital is continuously employed while another portion is used only periodically, in periods of peak activity. In theory, the former should be raised through the sale of securities, with only the latter provided by commercial banking institutions.

The practice is, however, often not in conformity with this general principle. Short-term borrowings are evidenced, it will be observed, by promissory notes, bills of exchange, and accounts payable on the books.

Fixed capital is supposed to be derived entirely from the investment market. In practice, however, funds for fixed capital purposes are often obtained from commercial banking institutions. In the past it was a common practice to borrow such funds on short-term notes which were more or less continuously renewed. In recent years such borrowings take the form of term loans payable in installments over a period of years. It is for this reason that a line has been drawn on the diagram between commercial banks and fixed capital.

Scrutiny of the fixed capital side of the diagram reveals that funds are transferred from ultimate investors to corporations by a number of routes. A part is obtained directly from the purchasers of corporate issues. Another part flows through investment banking institutions which handle the flotation of securities. Still other funds are assembled initially by intermediary investment institutions—savings banks, insurance companies, corporate trustees, and investment companies. As the lines indicate, such funds flow to the corporations either directly or through investment banking institutions.

Security exchanges, as shown in the diagram, are not in the direct line between the corporation and the ultimate sources of funds. That is to say, the securities do not pass through the security exchanges en route to ultimate investors, nor do the funds go from investors to corporations by way of the stock market. Thus the exchanges do not participate

INSTITUTIONS UTILIZED IN FINANCING CORPORATE ENTERPRISE

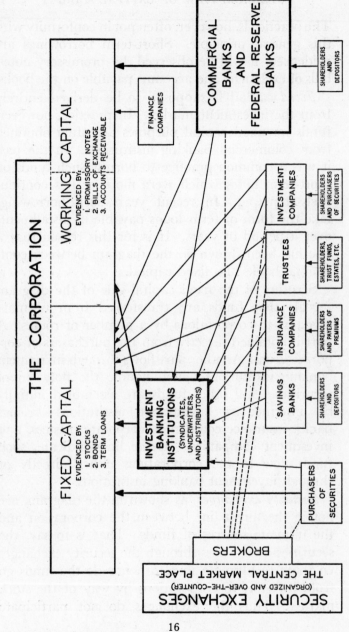

directly in the raising of capital. Their great function is to provide a central market place where securities already issued may be bought and sold.

The security exchanges are none the less of vital importance in the whole process of raising capital. If there were no market which enabled a potential investor of securities to get out—if for any reason he might wish to withdraw his funds—he would often hesitate to make the investment; marketability, or rather shiftability, is a very important factor. As we shall see later,[1] it would also be very difficult, if not impossible, for investment bankers to perform their functions without the security exchanges. This explains the connecting lines on the chart between the intermediary financial institutions and the exchanges.

The commercial bank is placed on the right-hand side of the diagram under working capital. This is because its most important function is that of providing short-term funds for operating purposes. However, as already indicated, the commercial bank also provides some fixed capital. Attention must also be called to the lines connecting the commercial bank with investment banking institutions and with the security exchanges. Investment bankers, when engaged in floating large blocks of securities, have commonly borrowed heavily from commercial banks, using these new issues or other securities as collateral for the loans. The dotted line drawn from the commercial banks to security exchanges is intended to indicate that the operations of brokers are facilitated by commercial bank credits.

The chart exaggerates the degree of specialization

[1] Chap. 3.

which actually exists. Although the major activity of commercial banks has been to supply short-term funds, in recent years—if public funds are included— by far the greater part of the assets of commercial banks is represented by long-term securities. Commercial banks, moreover, usually have a variety of departments such as the trust department and the savings department.

The inter-relationship between these various financial enterprises indicated by the chart should be stressed. The money market mechanism is not a mere aggregate of separate financial institutions. It is an integrated structure, possessing organic unity.

The money market is fluid and its structure frequently changes.

The chart may give the impression that the structure of the money market mechanism is a more or less final and definitive thing. Quite the contrary is true. New types of agencies frequently emerge to meet special requirements and conditions and establish themselves in the money market; Investment trusts, for example, were largely a development following World War I. Commercial paper houses and livestock finance companies, formerly important, have now virtually disappeared. In recent years commercial banks have established consumer installment loan departments and developed the serial payment term loan. A current innovation is the provision of credit pools to facilitate loans to business enterprises needing accommodation in excess of that which can be supplied by local banks. Changes in legal regulations force adjustments in the organization and in the practices of financial agencies. Until 1933 commercial banks were per-

mitted to have investment affiliates; but the Glass-
Steagall Act compelled a segregation of functions.

In the field of investment banking, as we shall see
in later chapters, the importance of the underwriting function has declined greatly in recent years.

*Fluctuating conditions profoundly affect the
financial policies of corporations.*

The striking feature of corporate financial policies
during the period of World War I was the great
reliance upon bank loans for expansion purposes.
Though nominally in the form of short-term obligations, thanks to the process of renewals and replacements, they were in effect continuous borrowings;
and the funds were used for fixed as well as for
working capital purposes. While the flotation
of securities was resumed in 1919, after the removal
of the capital market restrictions, bank loans continued to play a role of very great importance.

Industrial corporations eventually ran into serious
financial difficulties in connection with these bank
loans. In the boom period of 1919-20, inventory
speculation developed on an unprecedented scale.
Not only were large physical inventories accumulated, but advance orders for additional materials
were piled so high that the demand and supply situation in commercial channels was wholly distorted.
In the crisis of 1920 the drastic liquidation which
occurred centered in this inventory situation. In
money terms the inventory liquidation in the single
year 1921 involved losses nearly equal to those of
the three years 1930-32 inclusive.[2] This is explained
by the fact that in 1928-29 speculative activities had
centered in the securities markets rather than in com-

[2] *Federal Reserve Bulletin,* July 1941, p. 613.

modities. The liquidation of 1920-21 resulted in serious difficulties for both industrial corporations and commercial banks. A large part of the commercial loans proved to be frozen assets and could be liquidated only gradually. The process was enormously helped by the fortunate fact that the depression proved of relatively short duration.

In the twenty-year period which followed, two significant developments are to be noted. First, the indebtedness of industrial corporations to commercial banks was very greatly reduced. The corporations had learned from the grievous experience of 1920 that the maturing or calling of bank loans might threaten their very existence. They therefore sought as a matter of basic policy to lessen their dependence upon the banks for permanent working capital and to obtain the funds required, either from the flotation of securities or the retention of profits. As a result of this conception the relative importance of bank loans as a source of funds decreased considerably in the twenties, while in the thirties there was an absolute decrease in the amount of bank loans to business.

Second, it had become apparent that maximum flexibility in the handling of business financial problems could not be obtained so long as a substantial percentage of the capital employed represented bond indebtedness. Such debts involved not only the mandatory payment at set dates of fixed interest obligations but also maturities which might occur at unfavorable junctures. Common stock possessed a very great advantage in that dividend payments could be constantly adjusted in the light of changing economic and financial conditions. Even preferred stock gave more flexibility than bonds, since dividend payments could be deferred without forcing receivership; in the case of noncumulative issues they could be deferred permanently.

Accordingly, industrial corporations whose credit position was well established resorted increasingly to common stocks as a medium of financing. At the same time the gradual accumulation of undistributed earnings lessened somewhat their dependency upon the general capital market. In the thirties, as has already been noted, a combination of low volume of business and low prices served to decrease very greatly the over-all financial requirements.

The fluctuations in financial requirements and the shifts in corporate financial policies during the period which we have been reviewing indicate the danger of generalizing about the place of any particular type of financial institution in the scheme of things. At the end of World War I it was widely assumed that commercial banks would continue to play a dominant role in providing funds for industry. The shifts which occurred in the twenties led to the conclusion that security market flotations would henceforth constitute the most important method of financing and that the role of investment banking would continue to expand. In turn, the capital market stagnation of the thirties led many to conclude that both commercial and investment banking had had their day, and that henceforth business would be able to obtain the bulk of such funds as may be required from internal sources. This generalization, like its predecessors, must be modified in the light of the changes in financial requirements which have been brought by World War II.

CHAPTER III

THE DEVELOPMENT OF AMERICAN INVESTMENT BANKING

Some of the misunderstanding over the issues involved in security regulation arises from a lack of historic perspective on investment banking. In the course of its evolution, American investment banking has undergone many changes, and many functions formerly important are now of minor significance. Accordingly, if current problems of regulation and control are to be adequately appraised, a brief survey of the evolution of investment banking in the United States from its early beginnings until the present time is essential.

I. PRIOR TO WORLD WAR I

Though corporations were organized in this country during the colonial period few of these companies were industrial enterprises. Of the 335 profit-seeking corporations in existence prior to 1800, as many as 219 were turnpike, bridge, and canal companies, 36 water, dock, and fire companies, and 67 banks and insurance companies. Only 13 were ordinary business enterprises, of which six were manufacturing corporations.[1] The financing of these early business corporations was accomplished largely by subscriptions from the well-to-do merchant class, who were willing and able to assume the risks involved in new ventures. There was no attempt to raise funds from a "general investing public."

---

[1] J. S. Davis, *Essays in the Earlier History of American Corporations,* Vol. 2 (1917), p. 298.

Investment banking began as a side line to other financial operations.

The first stock exchange was organized in 1800 in Philadelphia and the New York Stock Exchange was organized in 1817. While these exchanges were developed to facilitate trading in outstanding issues, it was only natural that individuals with funds to invest should assume that stock exchange brokers might put them in touch with companies in need of funds. It appears that stock exchange brokers occasionally acted as direct intermediaries between borrowers and lenders.

In a similar way, concerns engaged in domestic exchange operations came to carry on a sort of investment banking business as a side line, especially in the purchase and sale of municipal and railroad bonds. They did not aggressively seek investment opportunities or organize selling campaigns. They followed the European tradition of waiting—or appearing to wait—for the investor to apply for subscriptions. It appears that they sometimes made investment suggestions to their clientele in their capacity as financial counselors; but this relationship was assumed only after the applicant had been properly introduced by responsible friends and acquaintances.

Among the concerns which developed along these lines were Drexel and Company, of Philadelphia; Brown Brothers, of Baltimore; Lee Higginson and Company, of Boston; and E. W. Clark and Company, of Philadelphia. In the middle forties the latter house, with Corcoran and Riggs, of Washington, participated in bidding for and securing the largest award of the Mexican war loans.

Before the Civil War investment banking in the modern sense was practically nonexistent.

The operations noted above were handled on an agency basis—that is, the bankers assumed no financial risk, guaranteeing to deliver to the borrower only such volume of funds as they might be able to raise in the course of time. They received their remuneration in the form of a commission on the amount of securities sold.

Security issues were then confined largely to railroads and other quasi-public enterprises, and to state and local governments. A substantial part of the funds required for these developments came from abroad, especially from England. Meanwhile American industry continued to finance itself chiefly through the re-investment of the profits of individuals and partners, or through the contributions of persons directly associated with the enterprises.

Public selling campaigns were initiated to help finance the Civil War.

This development is associated with the firm of Jay Cook. After serving his apprenticeship with E. W. Clark and Company, Cook established a banking house of his own in 1857 and became the financier of the Civil War. He organized high-pressure advertising campaigns in order to sell federal (and state) government bonds directly to the general public. In these transactions, however, Cook acted as agent and received a straight commission for his services.

Following the Civil War Jay Cook undertook to sell railroad bonds by the public-subscription method which had been successfully employed during the war. But he now adopted another principle: namely, that of purchasing securities outright—forming an underwriting group to take up any bonds which might not be absorbed by the investing public. The failure of Cook in the crisis of 1873 brought this method into temporary disrepute. It was, however, revived and elaborated, as we shall see, 25 years later.

The growth of investment banking paralleled the growth of large-scale enterprise.

The last quarter of the nineteenth century saw a very rapid growth of large-scale industry and the rise of the corporation to a position of dominant importance in the field of manufacturing. A rapid increase in national income occurred. Savings funds accumulated by the general public now became available for investment in business enterprises. This situation led to the organization of new investment houses and also the conversion of commercial brokerage enterprises into investment banking agencies. J. and W. Seligman and Lehman Brothers illustrate the latter practice, Seligman having been in the mercantile business and the Lehmans in the cotton trade.

A new method of selling bonds to the general public was developed in the early eighties. N. W. Harris and Company began the distribution of well-secured mortgage bonds through the medium of organized sales campaigns and widespread personal solicitation.

The Harris organization . . . was the first investment banking house which . . . sought to carry on a strictly retail merchandising business in bonds, and bonds alone. The Harris methods were ridiculed by other bankers who dubbed the Harris salesmen "bell ringers." But in the course of time every stock and bond distributing house of consequence has adopted the method of Harris. . . .[2]

It was not until the late nineties, however, that the investment banking business became a factor of major importance. Railroad reorganizations, made necessary by the panic of 1893, and the rapid expansion after 1896, necessitated flotations of a magnitude hitherto unknown. It was during this period that such firms as J. P. Morgan and Company and Kuhn Loeb and Company, with strong international backing, reached positions of leadership in the industry.

Modern underwriting developed around the turn of the century.

Prior to this time practically all corporate financing was conducted on an agency basis. That is to say, the banker undertook to find buyers for securities, but in case of failure did not agree to provide the funds himself. As industry grew in size, and the necessary funds could not be secured from family or acquaintances, the need increased for the services of a specialist in raising funds. What the businessman wanted was to be free to concentrate on developing and managing the business; he needed to be relieved from fund raising, a task for which he lacked the requisite experience. Special knowledge and an extensive organization was required to find potential investors and to convince them of the soundness of an enterprise. Moreover, there were serious risks involved for the company. What if investors in sufficient number could not be found? What if funds were not forthcoming as quickly as the

[2] Arthur S. Dewing, *The Financial Policy of Corporations,* 3d rev. ed. (1934), p. 961.

plans for business expansion required? *Underwriting* was developed in response to this need.

Underwriting involved an agreement on the part of the investment banker to provide the funds required at a given date. If unable to sell all of an issue during the time period agreed upon, the banker had to furnish the rest himself. In other words, he guaranteed that the corporation would have the "cash on the barrel-head" on the day stipulated.

During this period, in contrast to later practice, the investment banks which originated a flotation also handled the sale or distribution of the security. This was done either through its own staff or other agents selling on a commission basis. But to help carry the underwriting risks, the practice developed of enlisting the co-operation of other investment houses, insurance companies, commercial banks, and even wealthy individual investors. The rapidly growing size of flotations during this period made it necessary to obtain a wide participation in the assumption of underwriting risks.

Underwriting was made necessary by the relative dearth of investment money prior to World War I.

Throughout the nineteenth century and until after World War I, the volume of savings available for investment was inadequate to meet the expanding demands of business enterprise for liquid capital. As a consequence, a considerable time usually elapsed between the offering of an issue and the final disposition of the securities to the investing public. Frequently a year or two passed before an issue was fully sold. The banking group which marketed the securities of the United States Steel Corporation continued from March 1901 to April 1903; and an issue of the

American Telegraph and Telephone Company in 1906 was carried by the investment bankers for two years.[3]

In periods of very rapid industrial expansion, the volume of security offerings was greatly in excess of available funds in the hands of investors. Under these circumstances, the accumulation of unsold or partially sold issues reached huge proportions. The phrase "undigested securities" was coined to describe this situation.

It was the rule rather than the exception that the investment banks had to carry a substantial portion of the issues which they handled long beyond the date when the corporation obtained its money. In other words, they had to make good on the underwriting agreement. Without underwriting, the necessary capital funds could not have been promptly obtained.

The flotation and seasoning of securities were facilitated by commercial bank credit.

Since the investment bankers did not possess sufficient capital of their own to underwrite the growing volume of flotations, they found it necesary to borrow extensively from the commercial banks. Such loans were usually obtained by the pledge of unsold securities as collateral. The funds thus provided came in the main from the credit expansion which the evolving commercial banking system made possible.[4]

[3] *Commercial and Financial Chronicle,* Mar. 2, 1901, p. 141; May 2, 1903, p. 97; *Investigation of Concentration of Economic Power,* Hearings before the Temporary National Economic Committee, 76 Cong. 2 sess., Pt. 23, p. 12146.

[4] For a fuller discussion, see Harold G. Moulton, "Commercial Banking and Capital Formation," *Journal of Political Economy,* Vol. 26 (1918), p. 173.

The commercial banks also played an important part in the carrying of outstanding issues during what is known as the period of secondary distribution. It should be borne in mind that long after the investment bankers had disposed of a given offering it might still be years before all or the greater part of this stock had reached the hands of ultimate investors. In the case of little known or unseasoned issues, institutions and individuals looking for safe investments naturally preferred to wait until a corporation had proved itself. Such issues, however, offered attractive possibilities to speculators, who were interested not so much in a safe return as in the possibilities of market appreciation.

The activities of speculators thus served a very useful function in carrying, so to speak, untried securities until their investment quality could be demonstrated. The commercial banks once more played an important part in the process as lenders of funds to speculators. These loans were again frequently obtained by the pledge of the very securities which were being traded in.

The length of time in which securities, even of large, well-known corporations, continued to float around in the financial markets may be illustrated by the experience of United States Steel Corporation. Issued in 1901, as late as December 31, 1909, only 34 per cent of the common stock was in the hands of ultimate purchasers. By 1914, only 57 per cent was in the hands of individuals.[5]

II. AFTER WORLD WAR I

Following World War I the capital market

[5] For detailed figures for the entire period 1909-29, see J. Edward Meeker, *The Work of the Stock Exchange* (1922), pp. 584-86.

changed markedly. The volume of flotations increased enormously, in part because of the rapid expansion of industry and in part because of the desire of corporations to escape the vulnerability inherent in excessive bank loans. The railroads continued to be heavy borrowers in the capital market, but were no longer the dominant issuers. Both electric light and power companies and industrial companies became much more important than the railways. Financial and real estate securities were also sold in large volume, and foreign issues became a significant factor in the American capital market.

The source of the supply of capital was also greatly broadened. The public now placed a large volume of its savings directly in securities. This change in investment habits was stimulated by the popular distribution of federal bonds during the first world war. It has been estimated that before the United States entered the war about 2 per cent of the population owned securities and by 1919 about 15 per cent were security owners.[6]

The decade of the twenties became the great era of investment banking.

In this period the older houses expanded their operations by opening branches throughout the country, and many new investment banks were formed. More and more the commercial banks entered the field—through the establishment of bond departments and security affiliates. By 1930, commercial banks handled almost half the total underwriting of new issues and over three fifths of the total distribution.

[6] *Standard-Poor Outlook,* Aug. 28, 1944, p. 565.

During this period the process of flotation became a much more elaborate business. The great size of issues, and the nationwide distribution of securities—not only to institutions but to individuals—resulted in the development of a highly complex system. If one is to understand the basic problems involved in security regulation, it is necessary to distinguish carefully the several functions performed by investment banking institutions.

The diagram below may help to clarify the nature of the operations. It will be noted that there

FUNCTIONAL DIAGRAM OF INVESTMENT BANKING OPERATIONS

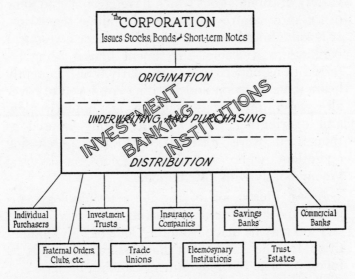

are three distinct and successive functions: (1) origination; (2) underwriting and purchasing; and (3) distribution.

The originating function may be broken into three separate operations: discovery, investigation, and negotiation. By *discovery* is meant finding a corporation desirous of making a flotation, or to whom the suggestion might be made that a flotation would be in the company's interest. By *investigation* is meant testing the investment credit of the prospective borrowing enterprise through the examination of its financial position and the condition of its physical properties. By *negotiation* is meant the processes which determine the amount, the price, and the terms of the proposed issue. For the services rendered in this capacity the originating house receives a special fee.

Underwriting and purchasing operations require very close analysis. The term underwriting carries a variety of connotations which have given rise to some of the most controversial issues in public regulation. It is sometimes loosely employed to cover investment banking as a whole—investment houses being referred to as underwriters. Similarly, one frequently hears the expression underwriting employed to cover all three operations—purchasing, underwriting, and distributing. Again, underwriting is used as though it were identical with the purchasing operation; while on other occasions, it is used synonymously with distribution.

As an illustration of the loose terminology employed by the investment banking fraternity itself, a citation may be made from the Code of Fair Competition for the Investment Bankers, which reads as follows: "The term investment banking business . . . shall mean the business of underwriting or distributing issues of bonds, stocks or other securities, or of purchasing such securities and offering the same for sale as a dealer therein, or of purchasing and selling such securities upon the order and for the account of others." It will be seen, first, that underwriting and distributing are used synonymously; and, second, that contingent underwriting is regarded as an alternative expression to outright purchasing.

The prevailing confusion arises from the fact that the distinct functions, originating, underwriting, and distributing, are so frequently conducted in the United States by a single institution. That is to say, a given house may originate an issue, assume the underwriting and purchase in whole or in part, and also participate in the distribution of the issue. Again, a house may perform two of the functions only; it may originate and underwrite without selling the securities; or it may participate in the underwriting and in the distribution without being involved in the origination. Thus the functional lines have been greatly blurred in actual investment banking practice.

In the distribution of a large issue, the first step was the formation of a selling group. This task was undertaken by the originating house, which had complete discretion in the selection of the members of the selling group. It naturally included such members of the underwriting or purchasing groups as desired to participate in the selling, but it included particularly a large number of retail dealers widely scattered throughout the country. The purpose of this large, widely dispersed selling group was to effect a quick sale and a wide distribution among ultimate investors.

The members of the selling groups as such did not participate in the underwriting agreement. They did, however, assume the risks involved in merchandising the amount of securities which had been allotted to them at a stipulated price. The members of the selling group derived their return from the discount under the uniform, public offering price allowed them by the underwriting syndicate sponsoring the issue.

The system of offering securities at a uniform price was developed in the twenties.

In earlier days, while the price to the corporation was fixed, the selling price to the public varied according to the conditions of the market and according to the negotiations of distributing houses with purchasers. When securities came to be sold in great volume and on a nationwide scale, it seemed essential to determine in advance the entire spread between the price received by the corporation and the price paid by the ultimate investors, and also the division of the differential as between the originating house, the underwriters, and the distributors. The operation of this system was facilitated by the greater supply of investment money that had now become available and the consequent shorter time period required to market an issue.

A stabilization procedure was developed to limit price fluctuations during the marketing period.

With the establishment of a uniform offering price to the public, it was highly important that price fluctuations during the marketing period should be at a minimum. Otherwise serious difficulties might be encountered in marketing the issue. The determination of the price at which an issue would be offered was often a difficult problem. The managing house naturally wished to fix the authorized price to the public as close as possible to the prospective market price at the end of the period. But a considerable spread might well develop because of a failure to gauge correctly the general trend of the financial markets, or as a result of market manipulation by speculators.

To safeguard the situation, the originating house adopted the policy of placing supporting bids in the market in the event of a decline, and of offering for sale undistributed blocks in case the market rose unduly. This problem will be further discussed in Chapter VI.

The enormous increase in investment funds in the twenties exerted a profound influence.

As a result of factors which need not here be considered, a fundamental change had occurred in the capital market situation in the decade of the twenties. Prior to World War I, as previously noted, the volume of money savings was relatively small and the supply of investment funds was usually much less than the volume of securities currently being offered in the markets. At that time some issues were marketed abroad and others, as we have indicated, were carried by means of commercial bank credit expansion.

The situation in the late twenties presented a sharp contrast. The volume of savings seeking investment outlets greatly exceeded the supply of new domestic issues, large as the latter were. Part of the surplus funds were drained off by the purchase of foreign securities, while another substantial part found outlet in the purchase of investment trust and holding company issues, the proceeds of which were devoted, not to the construction of new productive capital, but to the purchase of securities already outstanding in the market.

One result of this fundamental change in the relations of supply and demand in the money market was to reduce the importance of underwriting. The abundance of money seeking investment made it possible to dispose of issues within a very short period of time. Thus the risk of having to carry an unsold issue was greatly reduced. It frequently transpired that an entire issue was subscribed for by dealers even before the final negotiations with the corporation were consummated. This shortening of the time period also naturally simplified the problem of price stabilization.

A second result of the easy money market situation was manifest in the growth of competition in the investment banking business. As already noted, the flourishing character of the industry had naturally stimulated the organization of many new investment houses and an extensive invasion of the field by commercial banks. The resulting increase in competition lessened the relative importance of the houses which had been dominant in the prewar period. They remained, however, pre-eminent in the origination and management of large flotations.

The general market situation in the twenties also tended to modify the customary relations between investment bankers and corporations. Before World War I a corporation usually floated its securities through the same investment house year after year. While there was no legally binding contract, the investment banker commonly looked upon particular corporations as regular clients; the relationship thus tended to be continuous and essentially non-competitive in character. With the great expansion in the supply of available investment money and in the number of investment bankers in the twenties, the corporation became less dependent upon any particular house. New houses made aggressive efforts to win corporations away from their long-standing relationships.

At the same time, industrial corporations were becoming less dependent upon investment bankers in general. They were able to provide from internal sources increasing proportions of the funds required for expansion, and their own financial experts were in many cases equipped to gauge money market trends and conditions as well as the bankers themselves. In consequence of these factors, the bargaining position of the issuing corporation was much stronger than had been the case in the earlier days.

III. THE TRENDS OF THE THIRTIES

The dominant factor affecting investment banking in the thirties was of course the protracted depression. During the acute phase of the industrial crisis new flotations were negligible. Even during the partial recovery period which followed 1933, *new* issues for purposes of expansion were inconsequential in amount. On the other hand, the unprecedentedly low rates of interest stimulated *refunding* operations, designed to reduce financial costs. The chart on page 38 reveals the striking change which occurred between the twenties and the thirties. These figures, it will be noted, do not include foreign issues, which were very large in the twenties but virtually nonexistent in the thirties.

As a result of the great reduction in the volume of new issues, the amount of money savings, greatly reduced though it was, continued to be materially in excess of the demand therefor. In consequence, the easy money market situation prevailing in the twenties continued throughout the following decade. The basic explanation of the low prevailing rates of interest was the abundance of available investment funds as compared with the restricted volume of demand.

NEW AND REFUNDING ISSUES OF DOMESTIC CORPORATIONS, 1919-40[a]

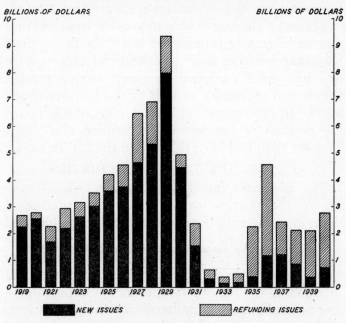

[a] Data for 1919-37 from U. S. Department of Commerce, *Survey of Current Business*, February 1938; for 1938-40 from the *Commercial and Financial Chronicle*, Jan. 15, 1942.

The dependency of corporations on the investment banker was further reduced.

Because of the abundance of available investment funds, security offerings could usually be marketed very quickly—once the conditions imposed by the regulatory authorities had been met. Hence the importance of the underwriting function continued to decline.

Moreover, the bargaining position of the corporation was materially strengthened. The reduced financial requirements, for reasons set forth in the first chapter, rendered the corporation much less dependent than formerly upon capital market flotations. At the same time, new sources of investment money became available as a result of the plethora of investment funds available in insurance companies and banking institutions. This situation gave rise to the practice of placing issues privately with institutional investors and of procuring serial term loans from commercial banks.

Private placements

While the term "private placement" is ordinarily used in connection with the sale of securities direct to insurance companies, and the expression "term loan" has been used in connection with borrowings from commercial banks, there is no essential difference in principle between the two types of operations. The commercial bank transaction is, however, usually handled on a serial repayment basis, while the direct placement with insurance companies is commonly payable in a lump sum at maturity. Term loans are in fact, frequently made jointly by insurance companies and commercial banks—the former taking the longer, and the latter the shorter, maturities.[7]

In recent years the volume of financing of this type is known to be large, but no comprehensive figures are available. The greater part of both the so-called private placements and the term loans have been sold to a relatively small number of large institutions.

---

[7] *Proposed Amendments to the Securities Act of 1933 and to the Securities Exchange Act of 1934*, Hearings before the House Committee on Interstate and Foreign Commerce, 77 Cong. 1 sess. Pt. 2, p. 533.

Over the seven-year period 1934 through 1940, about 92 per cent of the known volume went to twenty purchasers. As much as 60 per cent was sold to three large institutions, one company alone accounting for over 25 per cent.[8]

An interesting recent development has been the revival of the practice of acting as selling agent.

Instead of underwriting issues in the traditional way, there has recently been a tendency to handle transactions on a basis that does not involve the making of firm commitments. One type of selling agency operation is known as the "best effort" commitment. Under this plan the banker merely agrees that he will do the best he can to distribute the new issue at an agreed price. He does not underwrite the issue, but merely agrees to sell as much as possible and to turn the proceeds over to the corporation at the earliest possible date. The corporation and not the bank assumes the market risk. Under easy money market conditions, such a risk is usually not prohibitive for a large corporation of well-established credit position.

A variation takes the form of a *conditional* commitment. Here the investment banker undertakes to sell an issue at a stipulated price and to furnish the funds at a given time, but a reservation is made to the effect that the commitment may be terminated if unfavorable conditions should arise in the capital market. This is known as the "market-out" clause. This conditional arrangement was occasioned by the wide market fluctuations of the thirties and the uncertainties arising from impending war.

[8] The same.

These practices of the investment banker have probably been an important factor in influencing corporations to prefer private placements to public offerings. Unlike public offerings, no considerable interval of time is involved with private placements; hence there is no occasion for additional commitments. The corporation is usually given a firm commitment almost immediately after the terms have been settled and well in advance of the final changes. The corporation is assured that the funds will be available as soon as the legal details of the transaction have been completed.

IV. APPRAISAL OF CURRENT TRENDS

In the light of this background of analysis and discussion, what can be said with respect to trends in the capital market in the early postwar years? Are the investment banking practices now current likely to be continued, or shall we return to former methods? While no conclusive answer can be given to this question, certain factors of major importance in the situation are discernible.

In the first place, the expansion in over-all financial requirements indicated by the analysis in Chapter I clearly suggests that industrial corporations, generally speaking, will again be heavily dependent upon the general capital market for the funds required. The requirements appear to be so great that they cannot be financed from internal sources.

Second, it seems probable that we shall have no such redundancy of investment money as characterized the money market both in the thirties and the late twenties. The situation will be different from that of the twenties because of the reduction in high bracket incomes and the enormous increase in taxes

—both of which serve to restrict the volume of investment funds. The situation will be different from that of the late thirties in part because taxes will be higher and in part because the demands for capital funds will be so much greater. The stagnation resulting from low volume of output, low-price level, and retarded industrial expansion will presumably be gone.

The foregoing does not imply that we shall have a return to the situation that existed in the period before World War I, when the supply of investment funds was less than the volume of securities offered in the markets. It does mean a situation somewhere between the extremes of the period before World War I and that from 1926 to 1940.

In this situation, the dependency of industrial corporations upon investment banking institutions will doubtless be somewhat increased. It seems likely, however, that insurance companies and commercial banks will continue to make direct purchases of blocks of securities and to make serial term loans to corporations. Ordinary commercial bank loans should also show a great expansion.

Whether underwriting will assume a role of importance comparable to that of former times is, however, open to question. So long as the money market situation is reasonably favorable to the prompt distribution of security issues, it would seem that underwriting will not be of major importance. The underwriting practice was the outgrowth of a condition in which the supply of investment money was meager and in which the time required to dispose of securities to ultimate investors was long.

In any case, there can be little disagreement that one of the most important requirements of the post-war period is a healthy and expeditiously functioning capital market. Only thus can we hope to maintain a high level of employment and realize the rapid increase in productive efficiency and standards of living of which we are technically capable. The immediate task, therefore, is to remove any obstacles which prevent or retard the flow of funds into new capital investments. With this object in view, we turn in succeeding chapters to an examination of the government regulatory measures which have been adopted in recent years and of the controversial issues to which these regulations have given rise.

CHAPTER IV

THE BACKGROUND OF REGULATION

A variety of factors combined to usher in wide regulation of investment processes in the thirties. Oldest among these was the hardy perennial of fraud in the sale of securities. For decades, crooked promoters had had a field day with gullible investors who, greedy for large profits, were persuaded to buy shares in speculative oil wells and gold mines, in prospective real estate developments, and in perpetual motion contrivances. It is of course impossible to ascertain even approximately the losses to investors through fraud and deceit, though they undoubtedly ran into hundreds of millions of dollars annually. In an effort to reduce, and if possible to eliminate all together, crooked promotions of fraudulent securities, all of the states but Nevada passed so-called blue-sky laws. The same motives lay behind several early efforts to secure comparable federal legislation.

A second factor is an underlying distrust and fear of bigness in economic matters. This philosophy was reflected in the attitude of the late Justice Louis D. Brandeis and in the implications of the famous Pujo Investigation of the money trust in 1912. The big corporation is regarded as objectionable because of the power inherent in bigness. The investment banker is objected to because of the magnitude of his operations and his alleged control of credit resources. In this sense, the demand for control over the investment market and security issues is a reflection of Main Street's opposition to Wall Street.

A related basis for government control is that characteristic of the writings of William Z. Ripley and A. A. Berle and Gardner Means. Such writers were primarily concerned with the location of power and authority within the large corporation. They pointed out the devices by which control was concentrated in the hands of the corporate insiders; how the growth in the size of the corporation, the issuance of nonvoting securities, the creation of voting trusts, and the proxy machinery all operated to keep stockholders from exercising any power in the corporation. The result was said to be that there was ownership without power and power without ownership. In the main, the efforts of this school of writers were concerned with devising ways and means of developing responsibility by corporate insiders to the owners of the corporation's securities and of preventing the insiders from abusing their power and authority.

It is doubtful, however, whether any amount of literature of the class of Ripley's *Main Street and Wall Street* or Berle and Means' *The Modern Corporation and Private Property* would, in and of itself, have been effective in producing legislation, regardless of how skillfully it was written or of the care with which facts were gathered. The plain fact is that during the 1920's there was very little public interest in matters of this sort. It remained for events to bring the subject of regulating the machinery of investment to the fore.

The immediate stimulus to government regulation was the stock market debacle of 1929.

Legislators, who might have remained unmoved by academic arguments showing that practices in the securities markets were dangerous, were quick to

take account of widespread losses of the general public from security operations. It should be remem-
bered that the losses of the depression period were
general in character. There were losses to farmers,
to workers, to business enterprise. The crisis and the
loss of confidence, both in the United States and
abroad, were so great that the value of most forms
of property was necessarily reappraised downward.
That the reappraisal should be very drastic in the
case of securities, was inevitable, in view of the
character of the preceding speculation and the fact
that the existence of the organized exchanges made
it possible to sell out at some price. Where many
forms of property simply became unsalable or frozen,
the stock exchange continued to be a market despite
the extent to which prices declined.

The losses touched off by the economic setback
starting in 1929 followed a period of great activity
in which speculation was rife, bank competition was
keen, and investment banking rapidly expanding.
In a very real sense both investors and bankers were
actors in and creators of a speculative boom which
resulted in a situation highly sensitive to shock.

Once advancing stock prices get well under way,
they work to insidious ends. At the outset the careful and wise individual observes rising prices with
a jaundiced eye, but by degrees his perspective
becomes changed. That which was yellow becomes
green and stays green. Stocks which should not have
risen have gone up; they are still going up, up.
Everybody in the market seems to be making money.
Maybe, reasons the once cautious individual, I have
been wrong. The standards of the past do not apply
today; we are in a new era. Or, reasons another,

it may be basically unsound, but I'll get in, capitalize on it, and get out before the crash comes. Thus by degrees experienced investors, professional speculators, and the teacher, preacher, news dealer, and barber join to swell the ever-growing list of speculators.

Investment houses were increasing in number. The membership of the Investment Bankers Association, including main and branch offices, was 593 in 1918. In 1929 it was 1,902. By 1933 it had declined to 943. In 1942 it was 1,231, and in 1945 had increased to 1,342. Once the boom got under way, the conduct of the investment business reflected the speculative characteristics of the period. The over-zealous security salesman on the road was matched by an equally zealous sales manager in the home office.

At first many of the old, established houses stood firm in resisting the temptation to make large profits from quick transactions. They refrained from joining the crowd. But by 1929 there were few which had not fallen in line with the trend of the times. Such was the abounding optimism of the period that most of the cautious and careful felt that the situation might after all work out all right.

When the crash came, there was a widespread demand, as is always the case, for punishment. As usual this demand did not discriminate between the guilty and not guilty. The promoter, the professional market operator, the banker, the investment banker —all were in disrepute; all were regarded as speculators or "banksters."

Those who argued that many of the losses suffered were a natural consequence of a world-wide economic setback were ignored. Still others who argued

that regulation should be corrective rather than puni-
tive were considered apologists for wrongdoers. All
this is thoroughly understandable. That there were
many who were in no sense to blame was hardly a
thought upon which one could ask the public to
pause. The cry of fraud was widespread.

*It is necessary to discriminate between losses from
misleading statements and from market declines.*

It is easy for an individual to convince himself he
has been defrauded or deliberately misled when his
expectations are not realized by subsequent developments. Particularly is this true with highly speculative securities; and securities held by the general
public were usually of the more speculative type.

Most of the cases of outright fraud arose out of
the sale of common stock by the individual promoter.
In the field of stock promotion the twenties afforded
more than an average opportunity for an ambidex-
trous and shifty fellow—the stock swindler. His conduct changes rarely, his name and address frequently.
He had long since learned that he could put the law
off his trail by moving into an adjoining state.

There were numerous practices in the marketing
of securities by investment houses which were akin to
fraud. Bonds were sold that were bonds in name
only. Preferred stock, so-called, contained provisions
which permitted the withdrawal of preference rights.
Oftentimes the provisions were so complicated that
the buyer could not easily determine his rights. In
the public utility field, the device of the holding
company was used as a means of controlling vast
enterprise with scant funds and for the purpose of
escaping effective state regulation. Equities were
offered in investment trusts that had meager asset

values; the purchaser frequently had little more to rely upon than a blind faith in a list of dignified and reputable sponsors. Securities of foreign governments were sold which had behind them unbalanced budgets, a lack of foreign exchange, and a past history of revolutions and debt default.

The magnitude of the losses resulting from outright fraud or misleading information are unknown and unknowable. There is enough evidence to indicate that they run into large totals in speculative periods. One should, however, be on guard against the implications of statements such as the following:

When the buying mania began to spend itself in the fall of 1929, there was a tremendous market break. . . . The value of those stocks . . . continued to decline until in 1932 they amounted to a total of $15,000,000,000. This represented a dead loss of approximately $74,000,000,000 in about 2½ years. The market value of bonds on the New York Stock Exchange also decreased during that period from about $49,000,000,000 in 1930 to $30,000,000,000 in 1933.

. . . Here we see a capital market which in about one decade took the investing public for total losses of about $93,000,000,-000, roughly the difference between the high and low market values. . . .[1]

The use of the phrase "took the investing public" is itself misleading. It implies that all of the losses of the depression period were attributable to fraudulent or misleading information or manipulative practices. The statement, moreover, assumes that the all-time high of security prices in 1929 is a true basis from which to measure subsequent losses. As a matter of logic, if all the losses of the depression period are chargeable to the capital market, then all the

---

[1] Ganson Purcell, chairman, *Securities and Exchange Commission,* Hearings before the House Committee on Interstate and Foreign Commerce, 77 Cong. 1 sess. Pt. I, p. 8.

antecedent gains of the boom period should be credited to the capital market.

Statements which fail to discriminate between losses due to fraud and misleading information, on the one hand, and those which result from cyclical economic fluctuations and speculative excesses, on the other, can serve no useful purpose.

Information supplied purchasers of securities may be truthful yet not adequate.

In many cases the prospectus information, while accurate so far as it went, was so incomplete or unclear that the purchaser could not make an intelligent appraisal. This was especially true of investment-trust and holding-company issues. Information pertaining to the securities of medium- and smaller-size industrial companies was usually inadequate. In the case of real estate securities, the information was particularly unsatisfactory. With respect to foreign governments, the information was usually accurate and adequate so far as budgetary items were concerned, but inadequate as to the purpose for which the funds were to be used, the prospect of acquiring foreign exchange, and questions of political stability.

The information supplied purchasers by investment bankers during the twenties was usually adequate with respect to the older enterprises, such as railroads, operating utilities, and the long-established industries. The railroad issues were under the regulation of the ICC, and the operating utilities were subject to state regulation. The larger industrial issues had to meet the listing requirements of the security exchanges. These classes combined made up a large percentage of the total volume of outstanding securities. Notwithstanding such safeguards, these securities suffered severely in the general liquidation process.

The experience of the twenties clearly revealed the necessity for some regulation.

It is too much to expect that investors can always be protected against the excesses of their own conduct. Regulation cannot be expected to determine the explosive possibilities of all expansive periods at their birth, to anticipate the future, and to determine in advance what is sound and unsound. Neither laws nor men are that wise. Moreover, the attempt to do so would involve controls not only inconsistent with the survival of private enterprise but so detailed and cumbersome as to impoverish economic enterprise whether capitalistic or otherwise. Economic disruptions that destroy earning power inevitably will undermine investment value and bring bankruptcy and total loss in some cases.

It is not unreasonable, however, to insist that prospective investors shall be protected against fraud and that they shall be supplied with information adequate to arriving at an intelligent decision as to the risks they are assuming when they enter the capital market.

State blue-sky laws provided much valuable experience.

Before analyzing federal securities legislation, it may be profitable to glance briefly at the state blue-sky laws. These laws, as we have noted, have been adopted by all the states but Nevada, which announces proudly that it has no blue-sky law. The laws are of various kinds, often classified as (a) fraud laws; (b) licensing laws; and (c) registration laws.

A classification of this sort is becoming less and less valid as time goes on, since the tendency is for the laws to become more and more like one another. A fraud law may be amended to require a license, and a licensing law may be amended to require registration.

Fraud laws. Only Delaware, New Jersey, and New York have what may be called fraud laws. Such laws do not, in general, do more than provide for the punishment of those who engage in fraud in the sale of securities. Thus, the Delaware law provides:

Upon a verified petition filed by the Attorney-General averring that any person . . . is engaged in, or is about to engage in, the fraudulent sale or exchange of stocks . . . or other securities within the State of Delaware, the Chancellor may, in his discretion, issue a temporary restraining order, without bond, enjoining and restraining such person . . . from selling or exchanging or negotiating for the sale or exchange of any such stocks, bonds, notes, or other securities within the State of Delaware. . . . Any such person . . . may upon hearing be perpetually enjoined in like manner.

The New York law, popularly known as the Martin Act, and the New Jersey law are much more elaborate. Incidentally, the New York law requires the filing of a state notice which gives the name and address of a securities dealer, and a corresponding notice in respect to any security sold unless the security is exempt. In addition, the Penal Law of the state provides among other things for the punishment of fraud in the organization of corporations, for false and misleading advertisements, false rumors as to stocks and bonds, manipulation of prices, bucket shop operations, and the improper hypothecation of customers' securities.

Licensing laws. These laws place primary emphasis on the character and good repute of the dealer in securities rather than on the quality of the securities offered for sale. At the same time, licensing features may be combined with the registration of securities in a blue-sky law, or, as in the case of New York, a state notice may be required of the dealer though the underlying purpose of the law is to prevent fraud by exercising the power vested in the attorney general to bring suit to enjoin.

The Maine statute is a good example of a licensing law which contains some provision for passing on the qualities of securities:

Any dealer desiring registration shall file written application therefor with the bank commissioner, which shall be in such form as may be prescribed by the commissioner, and shall state the principal place of business, the name or style of doing business, and the address of the dealer, the names, residences, and business addresses of all persons interested in the business as principals, officers, directors, or managing agents, specifying as to each his capacity and title, and the length of time during which the dealer has been engaged in the business. Each application shall be accompanied by certificates or other evidence of the dealer's good repute, and, if required by the commissioner, a copy of the securities to be sold, a statement in detail of the assets and liabilities of the issuer of such securities, a statement in such form as the commissioner may prescribe of the general affairs of the dealer and issuer, copies of any mortgage or instrument creating a lien by which such securities are secured, a full statement of the earnings and expenses of each issuer for three years prior to the filing of the application, a copy of any contract to underwrite the securities to be offered for sale, the names and addresses of all persons holding ten per cent or more of the capital stock of the issuer, a statement in detail of the plan on which the business of the dealer is to be conducted, and such other information as the commissioner may deem necessary in considering the application. . . .

If the commissioner is satisfied that the dealer is of good

repute, and that the proposed plan of business of the dealer is not unfair, unjust, or inequitable, and that the dealer intends to honestly and fairly conduct its business, with disclosure of pertinent facts sufficient to enable intending purchasers to form a judgment of the nature and value of the securities, and without intent to deceive or defraud, and that the securities that it proposes to issue or sell are not such as in his opinion will work a fraud upon the purchasers thereof, he shall register the dealer unless objection to such registration shall be filed with the commissioner within the period of two weeks succeeding the publication of the dealer's application.

Registration laws. These laws resemble, in greater or lesser degree, the Securities Act of 1933 which is described below. In general, no nonexempt securities may be sold in a state which has a registration law, unless the security has been registered or qualified with the appropriate state authority. The distinction between the registration laws and the fraud laws is that the latter operate principally to stop activities already started and to punish the culprits, whereas the former are designed to prevent deceit from being committed.

Under the Massachusetts law, for example, the registration statement must give the name of the issuer, the place of incorporation, the general nature of its business, the purpose to which the proceeds of the sale of the securities shall be put, and:

The amount of capital devoted and proposed to be devoted to the business in question, with the number of and a classification of the securities issued and to be issued; the amount of the secured debt and the unsecured debt, with a brief description of the date of issuance, maturities and character of such debt, and the security, if any, therefor; and the authorized amount of capital stock . . . with the number and classes of shares into which the same is divided, and a brief description of the respective voting rights, preferences, rights to dividends or profits and rights to capital with respect to each class.

The Ohio law requires, in addition, profit and loss statements, statements of the prices at which the securities are to be offered, costs of financing, considerations paid by the issuer, and copies of advertisements, circulars, and prospectuses.

State legislation on securities did not provide an adequate regulatory system.

While the security laws of several states were reasonably good, the system of state regulation as a whole nevertheless remained defective. State blue-sky laws varied greatly in their coverage, in the kinds of securities exempted, in the details required to be furnished to the state, in the administrative machinery set up to enforce the acts, and in the extent of the discretionary power vested in the regulatory authority. The defects may be briefly summarized.

In the first place, even the most perfect statute is no better than the machinery of enforcement, and some states have been woefully inefficient in the matter of providing sound and competent administration. Second, the lack of uniformity among state laws makes it burdensome for nationally operating enterprises to sell their securities. Unless states make abundant provisions for exemption of out-of-state corporations, such enterprises would have to register in every state. On the other hand, if they were exempted from registration, the purposes of the legislation might be largely defeated. Most serious of the difficulties, however, is the fact that the individual state may enforce only within its own borders. It is a relatively simple matter for the unscrupulous promoter to set up shop in New Jersey while confining his sales to investors in New York whom he reaches by telephone. Under such circumstances, the most carefully conceived legislation is likely to fail in achieving its objectives.

The inadequacy of state regulation was doubtless of sufficient gravity to lead ultimately to federal legislation. As indicated above, however, there was no serious movement in this direction prior to the collapse of the stock market in 1929. Almost immediately following the crash, considerable agitation developed for restrictive federal legislation. Lengthy and detailed hearings were held by congressional committees into such matters as the Kreuger and Toll incident, the sale of foreign bonds, and the operations of the stock exchanges. Out of these, and from the investigation into the public utility holding companies which had been authorized as early as the Coolidge administration, there came ultimately the series of statutes administered by the Securities and Exchange Commission.

CHAPTER V

FEDERAL REGULATORY ACTS

Between 1933 and 1940, there was enacted a series of federal statutes which brought the securities markets and the field of investments under comprehensive governmental controls. Starting with the Securities Act of 1933, Congress passed the Securities Exchange Act of 1934, the Public Utility Holding Company Act of 1935, the Maloney Amendment to the Securities Exchange Act, the Chandler Act (Chapter X of the Bankruptcy Act), the Trust Indenture Act of 1939, the Investment Company Act of 1940, and the Investment Advisers Act of 1940.

I. SECURITIES ACT OF 1933

First of the major federal statutes dealing with securities and securities markets was the Securities Act of 1933. This act is concerned principally with original issues of securities. Indeed, except for the provisions of Section 17 which bar fraudulent practices in connection with old as well as with new securities issues, the whole statute deals with requirements governing new issues. It provides for full disclosure of all pertinent information with regard to a proposed issue, and penalties for violations of the act.

The statute is based upon the concept that truth has a great purging power.

The objective of the act as stated by the Senate Committee on Banking and Currency, was to:

. . . protect the investing public and honest business. The basic policy is that of informing the investor of the facts concerning securities to be offered for sale in interstate and foreign commerce and providing protection against fraud and misrepresentation.

. . . .

It is the conviction of the committee that these aims may be largely achieved upon the basis of fidelity to truth. Confidence must and may be restored upon the enduring basis of honesty with the public.[1] 49

It was believed that the requirement of "truth in securities" would operate to prevent the sale and purchase of fraudulent securities. It was argued that dishonest and "hungry" promoters would be discouraged from attempting to sell their "cats and dogs" by the ban on glittering predictions of vast profits, and the necessity of disclosing the nature of the security, and the disposition of the proceeds of the sale. It was thought that with access to all relevant information thus provided for them, prospective investors would be in a position to appraise the potential value of the security offered. Finally, the various investment services were relied upon to analyze and digest the data and make the results available to individual investors in simple non-technical language.

The act exempts only a few classes of securities and security transactions.[2] 50

Among the securities exempt from regulation are (1) issues of the federal government, of states or their political subdivisions, of government corporations,

49 [1] *Regulation of Securities,* S. Rept. 47, 73 Cong. 1 sess., p. 1.

[2] "The term 'security' means any note, stock, treasury stock, bond, debenture, evidence of indebtedness, certificate of interest or participation in any profit-sharing agreement, collateral-trust certificate, preorganization certificate or subscription, transferable share, investment contract, voting-trust certificate, certificate of deposit for a

and of banks; (2) notes, acceptances, and other types of commercial paper with a maturity of not more than nine months; (3) issues of nonprofit organizations of building and loan or similar organizations, and of farm co-operatives; (4) the securities of a common carrier subject to section 20 (a) of the Interstate Commerce Act; (5) receivers' certificates; (6) insurance and annuity contracts; (7) new securities "exchanged by an issuer with its existing security holders exclusively where no commission or other remuneration is paid or given directly or indirectly for soliciting such exchange," and (8) securities given in exchange under the condition set forth in section 3 (10) of the act.

Other exemptions were intended to apply particularly to small enterprises. By section 3 (8), the Securities and Exchange Commission is authorized to exempt issues which do not exceed $100,000 in the aggregate "if it finds that the enforcement of this title with respect to such securities is not necessary in the public interest and for the protection of investors by reason of the small amount involved or the limited character of the public offering." Another such exemption which applies largely if not exclusively to small enterprise is that contained in section 3 (11) of the act as amended which exempts "any security which is a part of an issue sold only to persons resident within a single State or Territory,

---

security, fractional undivided interest in oil, gas, or other mineral rights, or, in general, any interest or instrument commonly known as a 'security,' or any certificate of interest or participation in, temporary or interim certificate for, receipt for, guarantee of, or warrant or right to subscribe to or purchase, any of the foregoing." Sec. 2 (1) as amended by sec. 201 (a) of the Securities Exchange Act of 1934, 48 Stat. 905.

where the issuer of such security is a person resident and doing business within or, if a corporation, incorporated by and doing business within, such State or Territory."

A more important exemption concerns securities sold without the aid of the investment bankers. This provision was intended to apply only to small issues, which investment bankers do not commonly handle. However, many large issues have also been privately placed without the intermediation of investment houses. As a result, the term "private placement" is popularly associated with very large companies of national reputation.

Transactions by persons other than issuers, underwriters, or dealers are exempted. So, too, are transactions by dealers more than a year after the security was first offered to the public, unless the securities involved are part of the dealer's unsold allotment which he received as a participant in the distribution of the securities. Brokers' transactions on customers' orders are likewise exempt, though the solicitation of orders is not.

The required registration statement must disclose all pertinent information.

This statement must be signed by the principal officers of the corporation and by a majority of the board of directors and must be filed with the Commission before the mails or other means of interstate transportation and communication may be used for transactions in the security. If accountants, engineers, or other experts are named as having prepared part of the statement, their written consent must be filed with the statement. Two schedules are provided for in the law—one for domestic corporations and the other for foreign governments and foreign corporations.

Schedule A is the form used for domestic corporations. This schedule calls for the name of the issuer, the state of incorporation, the location of its principal office, the names and addresses of its directors, principal executive financial and accounting officers and, if it is a new business, the promoters; the names and addresses of the underwriters; the names and addresses of all who own more than 10 per cent of any class of stock of the issuer; the amount of securities owned by the directors, officers, promoters, underwriters, and principal security holders; the general character of the issuer's business.

The issuer's existing capital structure must be described in detail, including the types of outstanding securities, the number of each, and "a description of the respective voting rights, preferences, conversion and exchange rights, rights to dividends, profits, or capital of each class, with respect to each other class, including the retirement and liquidation rights or values thereof; . . . If substitution of any security is permissible, a summarized statement of the conditions under which such substitution is permitted" is required. "If substitution is permissible without notice, a specific statement to that effect . . ." is required. This reflects the influence of the Kreuger and Toll debacle.

Similarly detailed information as to the new security must be given: the nature of the security, "the specific purposes in detail and the approximate amounts to be devoted to such purposes," the estimated net proceeds, the price at which the security

---

[3] Sec. 26 (12).

is to be offered to the public, "and any variation therefrom at which any portion of such security is proposed to be offered to any persons or classes of persons, other than the underwriters, naming them or specifying the class," commissions or discounts paid, and the expenses incurred in connection with the sale of the security.

The issuer must also supply data showing its relation to the promoters and the principal stockholders. For example, it must reveal any amounts paid to promoters within two years of the filing, and the nature and extent of the interest of principal officers, stockholders, and directors, in any property which the issuer acquired not in the ordinary course of business, within two years preceding the filing, or proposed to acquire after the filing. Every material contract not made in the ordinary course of business must be described.[4]

Schedule A must be accompanied by or include a recent certified balance sheet and certified profit and loss statements for the three most recent fiscal years. If the proceeds of an issue are intended for the purchase of another business, a certified balance sheet and profit and loss statement must be submitted for that business as well.

The Commission, by virtue of its broad rule-making power, may add to or subtract materially from the volume of information called for by Schedule A. Section 19 (a) of the act, which authorizes the Commission to issue rules and regulations govern-

[4] "Any management contract or contract providing for special bonuses or profit-sharing arrangements, and every material patent or contract for a material patent right . . . shall be deemed a material contract." sec. 26 (24).

ing registration statements, and to define accounting, technical, and trade terms, provides that:

... Among other things, the Commission shall have authority, for the purposes of this title, to prescribe the form or forms in which required information shall be set forth, the items or details to be shown in the balance sheet and earning statement, and the methods to be followed in the preparation of accounts, in the appraisal or valuation of assets and liabilities, in the determination of depreciation and depletion, in the differentiation of recurring and nonrecurring income, in the differentiation of investment and operating income, and in the preparation, where the Commission deems it necessary or desirable, of consolidated balance sheets or income accounts of any person directly or indirectly controlling or controlled by the issuer, or any person under direct or indirect common control with the issuer. ...

And section 7 states that:

... Any such registration statement shall contain such other information, and be accompanied by such other documents, as the Commission may by rules or regulations require as being necessary or appropriate in the public interest or for the protection of investors.

Schedule B, used for registration statements by foreign governments and foreign corporations, calls for the following information: the purposes of the issue; the amounts and the character of existing and prospective debts of the issuer; any defaults which may have occurred within twenty years prior to the time of filing; receipts and expenditures; names of underwriters, authorized agents, and counsel; the offering price and estimated net proceeds; commissions and other expenses.

The Commission may refuse to permit a registration statement to become effective if it believes the statement to be on its face "incomplete or inaccurate in any material respect." In addition, if at any time the Commission finds that a registration statement, even though it has become effective, includes false or misleading statements or is incomplete in any material respect, it may after notice and hearing, issue a *stop order* suspending the effectiveness of the registration statement. In the operation of the act the stop order has been applied almost exclusively to the promoter; seldom against the investment bank.

The "prospectus" must meet standards set by the Commission.

The prospectus as defined by the act means "any prospectus, notice, circular, advertisement, letter, or communication, written or by radio, which offers any security for sale." It must contain such part of the data in the registration statement as the Commission thinks necessary, and the Commission may also require additional information. To protect the investor against the old device of putting painful facts into very small type, sec. 10 (c) (d) of the act requires that: "The statements or information required to be included in a prospectus . . . when written, shall be placed in a conspicuous part of the prospectus in type as large as that used generally in the body of the prospectus." Further: "In any case where a prospectus consists of a radio broadcast, copies thereof shall be filed with the Commission under such rules and regulations as it shall prescribe."

Unless it meets these requirements, the transmission of the prospectus through the mails or by any other means of interstate transportation and communication is forbidden. The act also forbids the use of these facilities for sending securities for sale or for delivering them after sale unless they are ac-

---

[5] Sec. 2 (10) of the act. This section also gives exceptions.

companied or preceded by a prospectus that conforms to the act.

The purpose of these provisions is to assure the prospective buyer of securities easy access to the more important information contained in the registration statement. This is necessary because the registration statement itself and the accompanying documents—although of great help to trained analysts—are of little practical value to the individual investor. He is not likely to secure a copy of the statement, but if he does, he most assuredly is not competent to understand it. More important, the act seeks to protect the purchaser against the glowing prospectuses characteristic of an earlier era, when half truths and even deliberate misrepresentations were commonplace.

The act provides various types of penalties for violations.

The act, as has been said, makes it unlawful to use the mails or interstate transportation or communication for dealing in or transmitting securities unless the requirements as to registration statements and prospectuses are satisfied. The Commission may seek injunctions to restrain violations. Willful violations and willful misstatements or omissions of material facts are treated as criminal acts, punishable by fine and imprisonment.

Most important of all, perhaps, are the civil sanctions. Under sections 11 and 12, investors who have suffered losses through material misstatements or material omissions in registration statements and prospectuses may sue every signatory of the registration statement to recover the amount of loss. The act places squarely upon the officers, directors, underwriters, etc. the burden of using reasonable precautions to ascertain whether the statements made are accurate. Even with the amendments of 1934, which lowered somewhat the standards of performance required of the signatories and added to their possible defenses in damage suits, they are still liable in civil actions brought under sections 11 and 12.

II. SECURITIES EXCHANGE ACT OF 1934

This statute with its amendments constitutes a logical companion measure to the Securities Act. The latter, except for the fraudulent practices barred by section 17 which apply to old as well as new issues, deals with requirements governing new security issues. Regulations affecting trading in securities *after* issuance are provided by the 1934 law. There are many parallels between the two statutes: both stress adequate disclosure of relevant information; both require registration statements; both ban fraudulent and deceptive practices and provide penalties for violation. However, the 1934 law goes a good deal further and provides for a greater measure of federal control than the older law.

According to the formal statement of policy contained in the Securities Exchange Act, regulation of interstate securities transactions on exchanges and in over-the-counter markets is necessary "in order to protect interstate commerce, the national credit, the Federal taxing power, to protect and make more effective the national banking system and Federal Reserve System, and to insure the maintenance of fair and honest markets in such transactions." The act goes on to say:

(1) Such transactions (a) are carried on in large volume by the public generally and in large part originate outside the States in which the exchanges and over-the-counter

markets are located and/or are effected by means of the mails and instrumentalities of interstate commerce; (b) constitute an important part of the current of interstate commerce; (c) involve in large part the securities of issuers engaged in interstate commerce; (d) involve the use of credit, directly affect the financing of trade, industry, and transportation in interstate commerce, and directly affect and influence the volume of interstate commerce; and affect the national credit.

(2) The prices established and offered in such transactions are generally disseminated and quoted throughout the United States and foreign countries and constitute a basis for determining and establishing the prices at which securities are bought and sold, the amount of certain taxes owing to the United States and to the several States by owners, buyers, and sellers of securities, and the value of collateral for bank loans.

(3) Frequently the prices of securities on such exchanges and markets are susceptible to manipulation and control, and the dissemination of such prices gives rise to excessive speculation, resulting in sudden and unreasonable fluctuations in the prices of securities which (a) cause alternately unreasonable expansion and unreasonable contraction of the volume of credit available for trade, transportation, and industry in interstate commerce, (b) hinder the proper appraisal of the value of securities and thus prevent a fair calculation of taxes owing to the United States and to the several States by owners, buyers, and sellers of securities, and (c) prevent the fair valuation of collateral for bank loans and/or obstruct the effective operation of the national banking system and Federal Reserve System.

(4) National emergencies, which produce widespread unemployment and the dislocation of trade, transportation, and industry, and which burden interstate commerce and adversely affect the general welfare, are precipitated, intensified, and prolonged by manipulation and sudden and unreasonable fluctuations of security prices and by excessive speculation on such exchanges and markets, and to meet such emergencies the Federal Government is put to such great expense as to burden the national credit.[6]

---

[6] Sec. 2.

Registration is required of all the more important security exchanges.

The Commission has power over all security exchanges. But it has been deemed expedient to exempt a number of the smaller exchanges from the operation of the act.[7]

To be registered an exchange must file a statement giving such information as the Commission may require concerning its organization and operation, constitution and by-laws, and membership. The exchange must also agree to comply with the act and the regulations issued pursuant thereto, as well as to enforce compliance by its members. Further, no exchange may be registered

... unless the rules of the exchanges include provision for the expulsion, suspension, or disciplining of a member for conduct or proceeding inconsistent with just and equitable principles of trade, and declare that the willful violation of any provisions of this title or any rule or regulation thereunder shall be considered conduct or proceeding inconsistent with just and equitable principles of trade.[8]

Registration is also required of securities listed on the exchanges, the information required being similar to that called for by Schedule A under the Securities Act. Further, the issuer of registered securities is required to keep the information current by filing periodical and other reports, as the Commission may require, in such form and manner and according to such rules as the Commission shall prescribe.

[7] An exchange may apply to the Commission for and receive exemption if the Commission finds that "by reason of the limited volume of transactions effected on such exchange, it is not practicable and not necessary or appropriate in the public interest or for the protection of investors to require such registration." Sec. 5.

[8] Sec. 6 (b).

The Commission may also authorize trading on exchanges in unlisted securities if there is available from registration statements and reports in respect to such securities

. . . information substantially equivalent to that available pursuant to rules or regulations of the Commission in respect of a security duly listed and registered on a national securities exchange, but such unlisted trading privileges shall continue in effect only so long as such a registration statement remains effective and such periodical reports or other data continue to be so filed.

The law seeks to prevent manipulation in any form.

A wide variety of manipulative operations is banned by the act. Pools, wash sales, matched orders, "touting" of securities, making false and misleading statements, and "creating actual or apparent active trading in such security or raising or depressing the price of such security, for the purpose of inducing the purchase or sale of such security by others," are all prohibited. In addition, pegging and transactions in so-called puts and calls, and other options must conform to the rules and regulations of the Commission.

Control is exercised over the flow of credit into the securities market.

Since this credit is largely derived from commercial banks, the administration of this section of the act is placed in the hands of the Board of Governors of the Federal Reserve system. Brokers are forbidden to borrow except from a source approved by the Board, and the power of the Board reaches even to the extension of credit by others than brokers or dealers.

The Board also determines margin requirements for individuals and stock exchange brokers.

Supplementary controls over brokers' borrowings are vested in the Commission which has power to limit the aggregate indebtedness which they can acquire to twenty times their net capital. In addition, the Commission is authorized to promulgate rules governing the mingling and hypothecation of securities. Brokers are also prohibited from lending customers' securities without their consent.

Various provisions of the statute deal with corporate "insiders."

The periodical reports required of issuers must give data concerning remuneration to officers, directors, and principal stockholders, and any other direct or indirect financial advantage or interest they have in the corporation. Further, the statute provides for the recapture of the short-term trading profits of such insiders in the corporation's stock, and prohibits the insiders from selling the corporation's stock short. In the same category is the provision of section 14 authorizing the Commission to prescribe rules and regulations for the use of proxies.

Very broad controls over the organization and operation of security exchanges are provided.

Thus, the Commission is empowered to prescribe rules for the segregation of functions of members, brokers, and dealers, for the regulation of floor trading by members, and for the prevention of excessive trading on the exchange, but off the floor. It is also authorized, where it finds that changes in the rules or practices of the exchange "are necessary or appropriate for the protection of investors or to insure fair dealing in securities traded in upon such exchange or to insure fair administration of such exchange," to request the exchange to make the necessary alterations in rules or practices. And, if the exchange should fail to comply with the request, the Commission may by rule make the changes.[9]

So sweeping is the control vested in the Commission that there is scarcely a single aspect of the operation of a securities exchange which is beyond the Commission's reach.

Criminal penalties of fine and imprisonment are specified for violations of the act, and the Commission may seek injunctions to restrain violations. The act also provides for damage suits by individuals who have suffered loss as a result of violations. In addition, the Commission may suspend or withdraw the registration of a security or an exchange, and it may suspend or expel from an exchange a member who has violated the act.[10]

III. REGULATION OF OVER-THE-COUNTER MARKETS

To deal with the difficult problems created by the over-the-counter markets and the multiplicity of brokers and dealers operating in such markets, the Securities Exchange Act was amended in 1936 by

[9] For illustrations of the kinds of changes contemplated, see sec. 19 (b) of the act.

[10] Under sec. 19 (a) (4), the Commission is authorized, "if in its opinion the public interest so requires, summarily to suspend trading in any registered security on any national securities exchange for a period not exceeding ten days, or with the approval of the President, summarily to suspend all trading on any national securities exchange for a period not exceeding ninety days." This is in addition to the power to suspend or withdraw registration.

the revision of section 15, and in 1938 by the addition of the Maloney Amendment which is now section 15A of the act.

One type of control centers on restricting mail facilities.

Under the first of these amendments, it is provided that brokers and dealers, other than exchange members, may not use the mails or the means or instruments of interstate transportation and communication for transactions in securities unless such brokers and dealers are registered with the Commission. Section 15 provides for the registration, sets forth the grounds on which registration may be denied or revoked, and prohibits fraudulent and deceitful practices.

A second method emphasizes self-policing.

The Maloney Amendment provided for the formation of associations of over-the-counter brokers and dealers along much the same general lines as those contemplated for securities exchanges. Standards are laid down for admission to and expulsion from membership in the association, and the Commission is authorized to order admission to, as well as expulsion from, membership. The rules of the association must be

. . . designed to prevent fraudulent and manipulative acts and practices, to promote just and equitable principles of trade, to provide safeguards against unreasonable profits or unreasonable rates of commissions or other charges, and, in general, to protect investors and the public interest, and to remove impediments to and perfect the mechanism of a free and open market; and are not designed to permit unfair discrimination between customers or issuers, or brokers or dealers, to fix minimum profits, to impose any schedule of prices, or to impose any schedule or fix minimum rates of commissions, allowances, discounts, or other charges.[11]

The importance of membership in a securities association is accentuated by the fact that members may not deal with nonmember brokers or dealers on more favorable terms than those available to the public generally. This rule seriously limits, if it does not altogether prevent, securities transactions by nonmembers of securities associations.

The only association to register under the Maloney Amendment has been the National Association of Securities Dealers (N.A.S.D.). The purposes of this association are broad. It is formed to promote the observance of the federal and state securities laws by its members. It is to serve as a medium for consulting and co-operating with governmental and other agencies on problems of interest to the investment and securities business. It is empowered to administer and enforce rules of fair practice and to prevent fraudulent and manipulative acts, as well as to promote self-discipline among its members.[12]

The association is nationwide in its scope. It includes 2,600 members, representing 90 per cent of all eligible dealers. Membership is practically mandatory for all active security dealers. Only members may participate in underwriting and selling groups.

The association has been effective in supervising quotations in over-the-counter securities. This work has been particularly important because of the absence of any mechanism for publicizing bid and

[11] Sec. 15 A (b) (7).
[12] Paul Grant, "The National Association of Security Dealers," *Wisconsin Law Review* (1942), p. 597.

asked prices. The association now furnishes quotations on unlisted securities, and these are quite generally carried in both the metropolitan and the local press.

Another function of the association is to establish and enforce rules of fair practice. Complaints from investors and dealers are received and scrutinized. In some cases these complaints have resulted in expelling, suspending, and censuring members.

The association has sought to strengthen the financial responsibility of its members. Such financial soundness is necessary in order to protect the security investors and also security dealers. The test of such responsibility has been determined by a firm's solvency or its net quick position. This must show that quick assets cover all liabilities. The net quick position should also be judged in relation to the value of the business of the firm. The first test can be readily applied, but the second is much more difficult.

The association also conducts an examination of its members. This is done by means of a questionnaire, and also by check-up through accountants or examiners sent by the association. The purpose of the examination is to study the financial position of the members and their methods of doing business, to discover any violations of the association's rules.

A difficult matter is the determination of what is a fair price. The association has the power to penalize a dealer if his price to a customer is not in line with the prevailing market. The issue here is whether the dealer is charging an equitable margin of profit on the transaction.

IV. PUBLIC UTILITY
HOLDING COMPANY ACT OF 1935

At the time of passage of the Securities Act, it was commonly remarked that the act tended to supplant the doctrine of *caveat emptor* with the doctrine of *caveat vendor*. The seller of securities would now be subjected to obligations which hitherto had rested, if anywhere, on the buyer. Still, there was nothing in the statute which specifically authorized the government to approve of certain types of securities issues and disapprove of others. Presumably, any issuer could attempt legally to sell any sort of security as long as he told nothing but the truth, and only as much as the Commission required him to disclose. Much the same was true of the Securities Exchange Act.

When we come to the Public Utility Holding Company Act of 1935, however, we encounter a statute with a much broader purpose. Here, as in the earlier statutes, there is an insistence on full disclosure of relevant information; there are also restraints on over-reaching by corporate insiders with appropriate penalties. But there is more. This act has as its avowed objective the elimination, so far as possible, of the larger holding companies in the gas and electric industries. In fact, this appears to be the primary purpose of the act, to which the other provisions are subsidiary. It is not too much to say that the act contemplates its own destruction, for if it is successful in securing the elimination of the holding companies, it will cease to have any significant function. The operating companies, it will be recalled, are controlled under other legislation.

*Public utility holding companies are required
to register with the Commission.*

Registration is accomplished by filing with the
Commission a statement containing specified types
of information, similar to those called for by the
Securities Act.

Nonregistered companies are forbidden to use the
mails or the means of interstate transportation or
communication for the purchase or sale of utility
securities, or for making or performing any service,
sale, or construction contract or to engage in any
business in interstate commerce. Registration is
therefore essential to survival.

The control over issues is broad and detailed.

Except as exempted by the Commission, in accordance with section 6 (b) of the act, registered
holding companies and their subsidiaries may not
issue or sell any of their securities or "exercise any
privilege or right to alter the priorities, preferences,
voting power, or other rights of the holders of an
outstanding security of such company," unless a
declaration is in effect with respect to the particular
security or transaction.

The Commission may not permit a declaration
to be effective unless the security is a common stock
or a secured bond or is intended for the purpose of
financing the issuer's business as a public utility company. These limitations, together with others contained in section 7 (c) of the act, would prevent holding companies from issuing debentures or preferred
stock, except for refunding or similar operations.
Operating companies would, however, be permitted
to issue debentures and preferred stock.

Further, if a state commission has jurisdiction over the security, as in the case of an operating company, the declaration will not be permitted to become effective if the state commission should inform the S. E. C. that applicable state laws have not been complied with. If the security is one permitted by the act and no state commission has objected to its issuance, the Commission shall permit the declaration to become effective unless it finds that:

(1) the security is not reasonably adapted to the security structure of the declarant and other companies in the same holding company system;

(2) the security is not reasonably adapted to the earning power of the declarant;

(3) financing by the issue and sale of the particular security is not necessary or appropriate to the economical and efficient operation of a business in which the applicant lawfully is engaged or has an interest;

(4) the fees, commissions, or other remuneration, to whomsoever paid, directly or indirectly, in connection with the issue, sale, or distribution of the security are not reasonable;

(5) in the case of a security that is a guaranty of, or assumption of liability on, a security of another company, the circumstances are such as to constitute the making of such guaranty or the assumption of such liability an improper risk for the declarant; or

(6) the terms and conditions of the issue or sale of the security are detrimental to the public interest or the interest of investors or consumers.[13]

Similarly, in the event of a proposed exercise of a right to alter preferences or voting rights of security holders, the Commission shall, in the absence of objection by a state commission, permit the declaration to become effective unless it finds that "such exercise of such privilege or right will result in an

[13] Sec. 7 (d).

unfair or inequitable distribution of voting power among holders of the securities of the declarant or is otherwise detrimental to the public interest or the interest of investors or consumers."

It scarcely needs to be pointed out that these provisions of section 7 vest in the Commission extraordinarily wide discretion over the kinds of securities which may be issued, and the prices at which and the conditions under which they shall be issued. By virtue of its powers, the Commission may, and does, shape to an increasing extent the financial structure not only of holding companies but of their subsidiaries.[14]

The acquisition of securities is closely supervised.

Unless the Commission approves, holding companies and their subsidiaries may not acquire "any securities or utility assets or any other interest in any business" (certain exemptions are listed in section 9 [c]). In applying for permission to make such acquisition, information concerning the transaction must

[14] Section 6 (b) provides for the exemption of notes having a maturity of not more than nine months and not exceeding 5 per cent of the total of outstanding securities. In additon, "The Commission by rules and regulations or order, subject to such terms and conditions as it deems appropriate in the public interest or for the protection of investors or consumers, shall exempt . . . the issue or sale of any security by any subsidiary company of a registered holding company, if the issue and sale of such security are solely for the purpose of financing the business of such subsidiary company and have been expressly authorized by the State commission of the State in which such subsidiary company is organized and doing business, or if the issue and sale of such security are solely for the purpose of financing the business of such subsidiary company when such subsidiary company is not a holding company, a public-utility company, an investment company, or a fiscal or financing agency of a holding company, a public utility company, or an investment company. . . ."

be given in detail. If there is no objection by a state commission having jurisdiction, the Commission shall approve unless it finds that:

(1) such acquisition will tend towards interlocking relations or the concentration of control of public-utility companies, of a kind or to an extent detrimental to the public interest or the interest of investors or consumers;

(2) in case of the acquisition of securities or utility assets, the consideration, including all fees, commissions, and other remuneration, to whomsoever paid, to be given, directly or indirectly, in connection with such acquisition is not reasonable or does not bear a fair relation to the sums invested in or the earning capacity of the utility assets to be acquired or the utility assets underlying the securities to be acquired; or

(3) such acquisition will unduly complicate the capital structure of the holding-company system of the applicant or will be detrimental to the public interest or the interest of investors or consumers or the proper functioning of such holding-company system.[15]

Moreover, assets or securities of a holding company or an operating utility may not be acquired "unless the Commission finds that such acquisition will serve the public interest by tending towards the economical and efficient development of an integrated public-utility system." In any event, the Commission "may prescribe such terms and conditions in respect of such acquisition, including the price to be paid for such securities or utility assets, as the Commission may find necessary or appropriate in the public interest or for the protection of investors or consumers."

Similarly, holding companies may not sell any utility securities or assets except in conformity with the Commission's rules or orders

[15] Sec. 10 (b).

. . . regarding the consideration to be received for such sale, maintenance of competitive conditions, fees and commissions, accounts, disclosure of interest, and similar matters as the Commission deems necessary or appropriate in the public interest or for the protection of investors or consumers or to prevent the circumvention of the provisions of this title. . . .[16]

Limitations are placed upon intra-system transactions.

Holding companies are forbidden to borrow from their subsidiaries; also, they may make no loans to them except in accordance with the Commission's rules. Limitations are also imposed upon dividend payments, and the Commission is authorized to prescribe such regulations respecting dividend payments as it deems necessary or appropriate "to protect the financial integrity of companies in holding-company systems, to safeguard the working capital of public-utility companies, to prevent the payment of dividends out of capital or unearned surplus. . . ." It would appear that the Commission may rule respecting every transaction between companies in the same system, since the language of the statute is indeed broad.

Especial attention is paid in the act to service companies. The guiding principle appears to be that not only shall engineering and mangerial service be performed efficiently, but they shall be rendered at cost. The Commission is authorized to issue rules "to insure that such contracts are performed economically and efficiently for the benefit of such associate companies at cost, fairly and equitably allocated among such companies." Provision is also made for the approval of mutual service companies

[16] Sec. 12 (d).

. . . so organized as to ownership, costs, revenues, and the sharing thereof as reasonably to insure the efficient and economical performance of service, sales, or construction contracts by such company for member companies, at cost fairly and equitably allocated among such member companies, at a reasonable saving to member companies over the cost to such companies of comparable contracts performed by independent companies.

The so-called "death sentence" was designed to enforce sound integration.

In the act's declaration of policy, we find that among other purposes, it was passed for the "simplification of public-utility holding-company systems and the elimination therefrom of properties detrimental to the proper functioning of such systems, and to provide as soon as practicable for the elimination of public-utility holding companies except as otherwise expressly provided in this title." The act contemplates the establishment of integrated public utility systems. As applied to electric utilities, an integrated system is one

. . . consisting of one or more units of generating plants and/or transmission lines and/or distributing facilities, whose utility assets, whether owned by one or more electric utility companies, are physically interconnected or capable of physical interconnection and which under normal conditions may be economically operated as a single interconnected and coordinated system confined in its operations to a single area or region, in one or more States, not so large as to impair (considering the state of the art and the area or region affected) the advantages of localized management, efficient operation, and the effectiveness of regulation.[17]

Section 11 (a) directed the Commission to make a study of all registered holding companies and their subsidiaries

[17] Sec. 2 (29) (A).

. . . to determine the extent to which the corporate structure of such holding-company system and the companies
therein may be simplified, unnecessary complexities therein
eliminated, voting power fairly and equitably distributed
among the holders of securities thereof, and the properties
and business thereof confined to those necessary or appropriate
to the operations of an integrated public-utility system.

As a result of such study, by section 11 (b) the
Commission was to require holding companies and
their subsidiaries to

. . . take such action as the Commission shall find necessary
to limit the operations of the holding-company system of
which such company is a part to a single integrated public-
utility system, and to such other businesses as are reasonably
incidental, or economically necessary or appropriate to the
operation of such integrated public-utility system. . . .

The Commission was also to require the companies

. . . to take such steps as the Commission shall find necessary to ensure that the corporate structure or continued
existence of any company in the holding-company system does
not unduly or unnecessarily complicate the structure, or
unfairly or inequitably distribute voting power among
security holders, of such holding-company system. . . .

In connection with this, the act outlawed the
great-grandfather holding companies—those companies which had subsidiaries which in turn had
subsidiary holding companies.

In order to effectuate the purposes of section 11,
the Commission was authorized to go to the courts
for an order enforcing its proposal. At the same
time, the act made provision for the voluntary sub-
mission by holding companies of simplification plans.

It was this section which aroused the greatest
opposition to the act, for understandable reasons,
since it entailed the dissolution of all the giant hold-

ing companies with their hundreds of millions of dollars in utility assets and securities.[18]

V. THE CHANDLER ACT

In preceding sections we have been concerned chiefly with the regulation of the marketing of new security issues and the sale of outstanding securities on the exchanges. The Chandler Act, now to be considered, is concerned with the improvement of procedures in connection with corporate reorganization. The circumstances or conditions which appeared to necessitate an act of this sort have been well stated as follows:

Under the old reorganization techniques, no effective devices were available for a disinterested diagnosis of the causes of corporate failure or for an impartial evaluation of the competence and fidelity of the management. Too often reorganization was founded on optimism rather than on an informed major premise as to the true prospects of the enterprise. The formulation of a plan, in most cases, was a prerogative of protective committees so-called. The right of individual or immobilized security holders to participate in the reorganization process or to receive vital information was circumscribed to the point of non-existence. Under the old equity receivership procedure, judicial scrutiny, if any, was of a minimal character. . . . True, 77B conditioned the approval of a reorganization plan upon the finding that it was fair, feasible and equitable. But this requirement was *brute force* from the outset, in that the statute provided no effective or appropriate procedure whereby the information essential to such a finding was made available either to the judge or the security holders. In sum, the enactment of

---

[18] The act contains numerous other provisions dealing with such problems as securities transactions by insiders, political contributions, uniform accounting systems, reports, investigations, employment of lobbyists and similar representatives, and penalties. These provisions are, in many instances, comparable to the provisions of the Securities Act and the Securities Exchange Act and need not be detailed here.

77B streamlined the existing procedure, but by-passed its fundamental defects.[19]

This act is designed to obtain disinterested analysis and advice with respect to reorganizations.

The act provides for the appointment of disinterested trustees who shall not be owners of the securities of the corporation in receivership; nor shall they have been underwriters for the debtor or have had any other relationship with either the debtor or the underwriter or any interest "materially adverse to the interests of any class of creditors or stockholders." The trustee is charged with the duty of investigating carefully the affairs of the corporation, of reporting to the court "any facts ascertained by him pertaining to fraud, misconduct, mismanagement and irregularities, and to any causes of action available to the estate," and of preparing a reorganization plan.

Two functions are delegated to the Securities and Exchange Commission under the Chandler Act. One, the Commission shall become a party to a reorganization proceeding if requested by the judge, and it may become a party on its own motion if the judge approves. In any event, copies of all reports must be sent to the Commission by the trustee.

More important, perhaps, is the provision of section 172 under which the judge, on receipt of a reorganization plan, may submit the plan to the Commission if the corporation's indebtedness does not exceed $3,000,000 and must submit the plan if the indebtedness does exceed $3,000,000. The judge may not approve a plan until after the Commission has filed its report or has notified him that it does

[19] J. A. Panuch, *The S. E. C. and the Chandler Act,* address before the New York County Lawyers Association, Nov. 21, 1939.

not intend to file. After the judge has approved a plan, the trustee must transmit to the affected security holders a copy of the plan, the opinion of the judge, and the report of the Commission.

The Commission is in a position to exert a powerful influence on reorganizations.

By becoming a party, the Commission can keep in intimate contact with the successive stages in the development of the reorganization plan and may thus directly influence the character of the plan to be submitted to the judge. While the report of the Commission to the judge is technically advisory only, by virtue of the fact that the judge is in no position to conduct a comprehensive financial survey of the company involved—whereas the Commission is fully equipped to do so—it would seem clear that the report of the Commission is likely to be decisive.

VI. TRUST INDENTURE ACT OF 1939

Another step in the extension of government control over securities was taken by the Trust Indenture Act of 1939. Various investigations of the operations of trustees under bond indentures had led to the conclusion that in numerous instances the trustee was unwilling or unable to take the necessary steps to protect the bondholders; indeed, the trustee often seemed less eager to look after the interests of the bondholders than those of the debtor corporation.

The purpose is to increase the responsibility of trustees of corporate obligations.

The act, which constitutes Title III of the Securities Act, declares "that the national public interest and the interest of investors in notes, bonds, debentures, evidences of indebtedness, and certificates of interest or participation therein, which are offered to the public are adversely affected" by the failure to provide a trustee, by the trustee's lack of adequate powers and responsibilities, by the trustee's lack of resources commensurate with his responsibilities, or by his having a connection with the debtor or the underwriter which "involves a material conflict" with investors' interests, by the trustee's lack of adequate information respecting the debtor's financial condition, and by misleading and deceptive provisions in debentures not fully disclosed to investors.

As in the earlier statutes, the main reliance is placed on federal control over the mails and on the commerce power. It is forbidden to use the mails or the means of interstate transportation and communication for transactions in bonds unless the bonds have been issued under an indenture which, in the case of securities registered under the Securities Act, has been registered with the Commission, or, in the case of other bonds, has been separately qualified. Applications for qualification have to contain information comparable to that contained in registration statements and, in addition, other information as to the trustee.

Various provisions in the act are designed to assure that the trustee under the indenture shall be willing and able to act in the interests of the bond-holders. At least one of the trustees must be a corporation with a minimum capital and surplus of $150,000. Further, the trustee may not be qualified if he has any "conflicting interests"; for instance, he may not be qualified if he is the trustee under another indenture of the debtor, if he is an underwriter for the debtor, if he controls, is controlled by, or is under common control with the debtor, if he is affiliated with an underwriter for debtor, or if he owns, directly or indirectly, more than stated percentages of the debtor's other securities. In line with these limitations, is the proviso that the trustee may not, except as permitted by the act, benefit by the preferential collection of his own claims against the debtor.

The act further requires that lists of bondholders' names and addresses be kept current and that such lists be made available to bondholders on the written application of at least three bondholders; if the trustee is unwilling to do so, he is required to distribute to the bondholders the information, proxies, etc., which the applicant bondholders wish to distribute, provided they pay the costs involved.

Regular reports must be made by the trustee to the bondholders in respect to the trustees' eligibility to serve within the terms of the act, their financial relations to the debtor, and pertinent information concerning the indenture and performance thereunder. Corresponding duties are placed on the debtor who must make available to the trustee periodical reports as to its financial condition and as to its performance under the indenture.

The indenture must also define what constitutes default and authorize the trustee, in case of default, to recover judgment against the debtor. Further,

The indenture to be qualified shall contain provisions requiring the indenture trustee to exercise in case of default (as such term is defined in such indenture) such of the rights and powers vested in it by such indenture, and to use the same degree of care and skill in their exercise, as a prudent man would exercise or use under the circumstances in the conduct of his own affairs.[20]

[20] Sec. 315 (c).

In the event an indenture does not comply with the provisions of the act, the Commission will refuse to permit its registration to become effective or to qualify it. Willful violations of the act are punishable by fine and imprisonment. Provision is made in addition for damage suits.

VII. INVESTMENT COMPANY ACT OF 1940

Of all classes of securities, those issued by investment trusts almost certainly had the sorriest experiences in the years immediately following 1929. Section 30 of the Public Utility Holding Company Act instructed the Commission:

. . . to make a study of the functions and activities of investment trusts and investment companies, the corporate structures, and investment policies of such trusts and companies, the influence exerted by such trusts and companies upon companies in which they are interested, and the influence exerted by interests affiliated with the management of such trusts and companies upon their investment policies. . . .

Following the report by the Commission, Congress enacted the Investment Company Act of 1940.

This statute resembles the Holding Company Act in many ways, particularly in the scope of federal control over the organization and operation of the corporations. It is also a very long and extremely involved statute, so that it is not possible to do more here than refer briefly to the types of control provided.

The principal objective is to secure honest, competent, and independent management.

Unless properly registered with the Commission, investment companies may not use the mails or any means of interstate commerce and transportation. In the registration statements, in addition to the information required under Section 7 of the Securities Act, the investment companies must give explicit information as to their policies in respect to specified practices such as borrowing money, issuing senior securities, concentration of investments, underwriting activities, and making loans. This information is quite important inasmuch as a company is forbidden to depart from its stated policies on these matters unless authorized to do so by a majority of its outstanding voting securities.

Section 9 (a) bars those convicted of crimes in securities transactions or those enjoined by a court from engaging in securities transactions from membership in the board of directors of an investment company. Also, a company may not employ as regular broker, or as underwriter, any of its directors unless a majority of the board are not affiliated with the broker or the underwriter. An investment banker may not serve as director unless a majority of the board are not investment bankers, nor may a majority of the board consist of persons who are officers or directors of any one bank. No person may serve as director unless he has been duly elected by the stockholders.

A wide variety of functions and activities are brought under control by the act. Among these are regulations as to minimum size of investment companies, concentration of investments, the employment of investment advisers, the circumstances under which senior securities may be issued, limitations as to dividend payments, the use of proxies, making available to stockholders the lists of stockholders to facilitate communication by discontented security owners, voting trusts, loans, distributions, redemption and repurchase of senior securities, circular and cross-ownership, etc. Appropriate penalties are provided for violations.

It is interesting to observe that the statute does not provide for the dissolution of the very large units after the fashion of the Public Utility Holding Company Act. Assuredly, however, every economic reason which justified simplification in the case of the latter was present in the case of the investment companies. Yet, the Investment Company Act provides merely for limitations on future pyramiding of investment company systems by the proviso that a company shall not buy the stock of other investment companies of which it owns less than 25 per cent unless as a result of the purchase it will own not more than 5 per cent of the outstanding securities of the company. This permits movement toward complete ownership of already partly owned companies while inhibiting expansion into other companies.

VIII. INVESTMENT ADVISERS ACT OF 1940

In the late twenties and especially in the early thirties, in response to a demand for an independent advisory and managerial service, there developed a considerable number of so-called investment counselors specializing in the handling of large individual and institutional accounts. Title II of the Investment Company Act, known as the Investment Advisers Act, was designed to control the activities of these investment counselors.

This act subjects investment counselors to public control.

The Investment Advisers Act prohibits, to all but specifically exempted investment advisers, the use of the mails and interstate transportation and communication facilities. The principal exemptions are those whose only clients are investment and insurance companies and those with fewer than 15 clients who do not represent themselves as general investment advisers.

Investment advisers must register with the Commission, giving information as to their organization and operation, their education and qualifications, nature and scope of authority with respect to clients' funds, etc. The Commission may refuse registration or withdraw it in the event that the investment adviser has been guilty of violations in respect to securities transactions or laws regulating securities.

Investment advisers are forbidden to enter into contracts providing for their remuneration on the basis of a percentage of the appreciation of clients' funds. Moreover, they may not assign their investment advisory contracts without the clients' consent.

The prohibitions of section 17 of the Securities Act are extended to investment advisers. They may neither "employ any device, scheme, or artifice to defraud any client or prospective client," nor "engage in any transaction, practice, or course of business which operates as a fraud or deceit upon any client or prospective client." Further, if in any transaction for a client, the adviser is acting as a broker or as a principal, he is required to inform the client as to the capacity in which he is operating. Penalties of fine and imprisonment are provided for willful violations of the act.

CHAPTER VI

THE ISSUES

A federal security regulatory system, revolutionary in character and comprehensive in scope, could scarcely fail to give rise to bitter controversy. At the outset the Commission reflected the view that the great depression of 1929-33 was primarily the result of financial misconduct. With a crusading zeal, government administrators sought not only to prevent fraudulent practices, but to eliminate the risk element in security operations—to prevent losses to the investing public. On the other side, those whose business was now subjected to regulation frequently found no good in the act. There were many who contended that the regulatory system so severely impeded the flow of funds into capital investment as to undermine the foundations of economic progress.

With the passage of time, with changing administrative personnel, with modifications of administrative procedures, and with a growing recognition on the part of the financial community that only by means of federal regulation could fraudulent promoters and irresponsible dealers be eliminated, the area of disagreement has been greatly narrowed. It is now generally accepted that adequate self-control by the industry alone is impossible and that regulation is an essential safeguard to legitimate investment banking. The problem is now conceived to be the removal of certain defects in legislation and the improvement of administrative procedures with a view to safeguarding the interest of the public without unnecessarily handicapping the operations of the investment banking and security exchange system.

The principal issues requiring discussion may be succinctly stated as follows:

Should regulation go beyond preventing fraud and requiring adequate information?

Should competitive bidding be required for all classes of issues?

Should stabilization operations during the period of flotation be permitted?

Should the several investment banking functions be segregated?

Is private placement desirable?

Should the investment banking system be decentralized?

How can security legislation be simplified?

How can the registration procedure be improved?

What changes should be made in the waiting period?

What should be the liability under security legislation?

Each of these issues requires analysis in the light of the discussion of the preceding chapters and of experience under the existing regulatory system.

I. SHOULD REGULATION GO BEYOND PREVENTING FRAUD AND REQUIRING ADEQUATE INFORMATION?

Concerning the desirablility of eliminating fraud, there has never been any disagreement. Numerous state laws, as we have seen, were specifically designed to curb the sale of fraudulent issues. This was also a primary purpose of the Federal Securities Act of 1933; and it is clearly within the province of the Securities and Exchange Commission to prevent the sale of fraudulent issues. The public must be protected from downright misstatements of fact. The S.E.C. has, in fact, been highly successful in preventing the flotation of fraudulent issues. Operators of bucket shops, outright swindlers, and dispensers of dishonest promotional literature have been harried out of business.

The public has also been safeguarded from misleading information in the form of statements which may be literally correct but represent only half truths. Again, there is no real difference of view as to the importance of providing the investing public with *adequate* information with respect to new security issues. Just how comprehensive the financial statements and other supporting evidence must be in order to permit the investor to make an intelligent judgment is, however, in the nature of the case open to some difference of opinion. In its efforts to make sure that adequate information is available, the Commission has required the preparation of very extensive reports. These have often been unnecessarily detailed; and they have frequently been burdensome, especially to smaller companies. The only question at issue here pertains to the amount and character of the information required; there is no disagreement as to the necessity of furnishing adequate data.

The basic issue with respect to the scope of the regulatory power is whether the Securities and Exchange Commission should pass on the soundness or probable safety of new security flotations. As we have seen, the security legislation was a result of agitation occasioned by the vast security losses occurring during the depression of 1929-33. Nevertheless, the Securities Act of 1933 was clearly not designed to have the government guarantee the

soundness of security issues. This act, it will be recalled, related both to industrial and public utility
companies. In recommending the act to Congress,
President Roosevelt said: "The Federal Government
cannot and should not take any action which might
be construed as approving or guaranteeing that
newly issued securities are sound in the sense that
their value will be maintained or that the properties
which they represent will earn profit." [1] The wording
of the law itself bears out this point of view. Moreover, the Federal Trade Commission, in administering the act before the S.E.C. was formed, recognized
this principle. The prospectus under the Securities
Act carries this statement: "It is a criminal offense to
represent that the Commission has approved these
securities or has made any findings that the statements in this prospectus or in the registration statement are correct."

Nevertheless, the Commission was so bent upon
protecting the public that in practice there was a
tendency on the part of zealous administrators to
prevent the flotation of securities whose ultimate
soundness might be in doubt. By the protracted
use of letters of deficiency and stop orders, it was
possible to prevent the flotation of securities where
the risk element appeared large. One finds in the
official explanation for the issuance of stop orders,
statements which suggest that the Commission was
at times concerned not only with fraud and complete
information but also with the safety or probable
stability of the security in question.

It appears also that the administrators of the act

[1] *Federal Supervision of Traffic in Investment Securities in Interstate Commerce,* Report of the House Committee on Interstate and
Foreign Commerce, H. Rept. 85, 73 Cong. 1 sess., pp. 1, 2.

have not infrequently exerted a direct influence upon corporate policies even where no question of fraudulent statements or inadequate information was involved. The nature of the powers sometimes assumed by the administrators has been well stated by a former prominent member of the staff in the following description of registration procedure: "If the need of the registrant is sufficiently urgent, a trade may be consummated. In return for the favor of the administrator, the registrant may amend its practices in accordance with the administrator's conception of equity and justice." [2]

The Commission has also apparently expressed sweeping judgments on the financial status of corporations. For example, it is declared that a certain utility was "little more than a set of books"; that a particular industrial company might as well quit business; that a toll bridge company would be bankrupt after the proposed reorganization plan went into effect; and that another company was an "incubator for future reorganizations." [3]

In contrast with the principle underlying the Securities Act of 1933 that the function of the government is merely to prevent fraud and ensure adequate information, the Public Utility Holding Company Act of 1935 specifically authorizes the Securities and Exchange Commission to pass upon the soundness of securities. Under this act, which relates only to holding company systems in the public utility field, the Commission has exerted a decisive influence upon the financial and managerial policies of such

[2] Abe Fortas, "The Securities Act and Corporate Reorganizations," 4 *Law and Contemporary Problems* 239 (1937).

[3] Hiram L. Jome, "The New Schoolmaster in Finance," 40 *Michigan Law Review* 643-44. (1942).

corporations. The Commission in effect writes the indenture and determines the provisions of the issue. It examines the capital structure of the borrowing corporation (section 7 [d] subsection [1]) and in effect establishes specific ratios for the proportions of funded debt, preferred stock, and common stock to total capitalization (section 7 [d] subsection [2]). The act itself envisages capital structures that will ensure "reasonable" coverages of interest and preferred dividends. In one case the Commission expressed the opinion that the company has an extremely unhealthy capitalization and that the proposed plan will not result in any material betterment of its structure.[4]

The Commission has so interpreted the Public Utility law as to give it the power to pass upon the purposes to which the proceeds of any issue are applied.[5] The Commission contends that it has this discretionary power under section 7 (d) (3) which states that the financing must be necessary and appropriate to the economical and efficient operation of the company. The Commission has power to prescribe what dividends a corporation may disburse, and what reserves it may set aside.

The Commission also passes judgment upon the relative worth of different issues. For example, in 1944 the United Corporation, as a step in the liquidation of its holdings, offered to its preferred stockholders for each share an exchange of 1.8 shares of Philadelphia Electric and $5 in cash. The holding of hearings and study of the plan involved nearly five months of waiting. Finally the plan was accepted

[4] Iowa Public Service Company, 1 S.E.C. 959-62 (1936).
[5] Northern State Power Co., 2 S.E.C. 825 (1937).

by the S.E.C. but with the stipulation that, instead of $5 in cash, $6 should be given for each preferred share surrendered. This was perforce accepted by the company. Again, in 1945 United Corporation offered two shares of Delaware Power and Light and $5 in cash for each preferred stock surrendered for cancellation. The process of discussion took over three months. The S.E.C. approved the offer with the condition that instead of $5 in cash $6 be given for each preferred share surrendered.

In these cases many months of delay were involved in the process of substituting the judgment of the S.E.C. as to the probable worth of the securities involved for the respective judgments of the United Corporation and its preferred stockholders. It should be borne in mind that no question of fraud was involved and that full information was available. The United Corporation preferred stockholders were free to accept or not accept the terms offered, according to their best judgment. No one was being compelled to part with his securities.

It is of interest to note that in the first of these cases the judgment of the Commission was not subsequently confirmed by market trends. The important point, however, is not whether the Commission's judgment happens to be good or bad in the particular case. The basic issues are: (1) whether there is any necessity of taking several months for reaching a decision; and (2) whether in any event the S.E.C. should substitute its judgment as to relative values for that of the corporation and the investors in a situation where information is truthful and adequate and where the stockholders are free either to accept or reject the exchange offered by management.

It should be noted at this place that in the railroad field the I.C.C. had long been vested with authority over the financial operations of railway companies. In the exercise of its power the Commission only required truthful and complete reports relating to new issues but to many it seemed to give virtual assurance to the public as to the investment quality of the issue. The St. Louis and San Francisco bond issue of the late twenties may be cited as a case in point. However, in the light of chastening experience the Commission has in late years repudiated any such policy.

Conclusion ✓

The government should not pass upon the soundness of security issues. The only safe principle for the government to follow is embodied in the Securities Act of 1933. The moment the government expresses a judgment as to soundness, it assumes a moral if not a legal responsibility to protect the investor from subsequent loss. Moreover, the assumption of such a responsibility inevitably leads to the following results: (1) it greatly increases the time involved in reaching decisions and hence in providing the funds required by the issuing corporation; (2) it necessitates extensive control by the government over the financial and managerial decisions of business enterprises; and (3) it restricts flotations to issues involving a minimum element of risk, thereby hampering the development of new enterprises through the use of venture capital.

II. SHOULD COMPETITIVE BIDDING BE REQUIRED FOR ALL CLASSES OF ISSUES?

Considerable controversy has developed over the methods of negotiating a new issue. It may be negotiated either on a private noncompetitive basis or by open competition. The private noncompetitive method involves a sort of partnership between the corporation and the investment bank; open competition implies only a temporary relationship for a particular transaction.

Certain advantages are claimed for the noncompetitive system—also called the *closed* system. The investment banker who serves a corporation continuously over a period of years tends to become intimately acquainted with all phases of the company's business. The banking house is thus in an advantageous position to give advice on financial policy. Moreover, since the investment house need not fear losing the issue by postponing its flotation, it is better able to *time* the issue and obtain the most favorable market.

The noncompetitive system, it is contended, also brings advantages to the investor. By virtue of the closed relationship between the borrowing corporation and the investment banker, the latter becomes in a sense "sponsor" for the issue. The banker does not, however, guarantee the investor that the interest or dividend will be paid, or that the security will appreciate in price. But the banker is in position to give assurance with respect to the fairness of the sales price in relation to underlying values and also to the safeguards in the terms of the investment contract.

The competitive system is supported on two principal grounds: The first is that it ensures the corporation's obtaining the best possible price. Competition among investment houses leads to close figuring, and it may be presumed that the business will thus go to the most efficient.

The second argument in favor of the competitive system is that it prevents the possibility of banker *domination* of corporate policies. In short, one of the alleged advantages of the closed relationship is held to be subject to grave abuse—for the banker may become not merely the merchandiser of securities but also in effect the manager of the corporation, dictating business as well as financial policies. It was chiefly because of this fear that federal and state legislation made the open relationship mandatory in certain types of financing, notably in railroad equipment and some classes of public utility issues.

Two comments are in order with respect to the alleged advantages of the competitive or open system. First, as to cost it sometimes works out in practice that a bidder, in order to be successful, makes his bid too high; and he is then forced to offer it to the public at a price higher than would otherwise prevail. The gain to the corporation may thus be at the expense of the buyer. However, there has not as yet been sufficient experience to warrant any general conclusion as to the relative cost under the two methods.

Second, the fear of domination of corporate policies was not without some basis in the period when investment money was relatively scarce and the services of the investment banker indispensable. Since investment bankers were often likely to be more interested in the conservation of existing assets than in the creation of new ones through the processes of expansion, the banker influence was not always economically advantageous. But under present conditions, with corporations possessing financial experts of their own and having ready access to alternative sources of funds, there appears to be little danger of domination by the investment banker.

Competitive bidding should not be compulsory for all types of issues. No hard and fast rule can be laid down with respect to the relative advantages of the open and closed system. Whether competitive or noncompetitive negotiation is the better method depends upon circumstances. It would seem that the noncompetitive system is preferable in the case of large and complicated issues where the terms require careful analysis and in the case of corporations whose credit position is not well established. On the other hand, competitive bidding may be used advantageously for issues where the terms are well standardized and where the corporation's financial standing is of the highest. For this reason we would oppose a legal provision making competitive bidding mandatory for all types of issues.

III. SHOULD STABILIZATION DURING THE FLOTATION PERIOD BE PERMITTED?

One of the most controversial issues between the investment bankers and the Commission has been over the right of the former to undertake stabilization operations. These operations are undertaken by the investment banker in order to reduce the variation between the fixed offering price of a new issue and its actual market price. As a rule these operations continue during the initial distribution period, after which it is assumed the issue is able to stand on its own feet. The most common method of support is for the syndicate manager to place bids in the market at or close to the public offering price.

This system of distribution at a fixed public offering price and the stabilization of an issue around this
price has come to be a generally accepted practice
of the American capital market for the flotation of
a new issue. The fixed offering price device is an
integral part of the stabilization system; there can
be no stabilization unless there is a fixed offering
price.

In recent years administrators of securities legislation have criticized the use of the fixed offering price
and stabilizaton. It is held that all forms of stabilization are unsound, that in every case such operations
are unjustified. It is contended that an artificial price
is deceptive and works against the interest of the
investor; that stabilization results in overpricing and
that after stabilization, prices generally drop, bringing serious loss to the investor. Stabilization is regarded as interfering with a free and open market.
From the legal standpoint, it has been asserted that
stabilization may operate as a restraint of trade, thus
bringing bankers within the provisions of the anti-
trust act. It is also pointed out that in the British
capital market stabilization operations are not conducted, and securities from the outset are permitted
to seek their own level of value.

The contention that stabilization results in overpricing and consequently loss to the investor has not
been supported by actual studies on this subject. A
comprehensive survey of the market action of new
bond issues shows that a large majority have had a
satisfactory experience in the period immediately
following their distribution. The study included an
analysis of the market behavior of 401 bonds with a

par value of over 12 billion dollars.[6] In 85 per cent of these cases the investor could have sold his holdings at a profit within a year after the purchase of the bonds.

Investment bankers maintain that this system enables corporations to obtain their funds at a lower cost than they would receive in a free market. It is held that the risks involved in the flotation of an issue without a fixed price device and stabilization would be so great that the investment banker would be forced to pass on the premium for such a risk by increasing the cost of capital to the corporation.

There is undoubtedly real value in stabilizing operations because of the market uncertainties with which new issues are inevitably surrounded. In consequence they invite operations by speculators interested in short-term profits. In the absence of market support, wide oscillations disturbing alike to the corporation, the investment banker, and the investor might occur.

Granting that stabilization normally serves a useful function in minimizing speculative influences, it is still possible that abuses may enter through maintaining a price wholly out of line with market realities. Carried to extremes the supporting of a security might evolve into holding a price on the exchange so out of line with investment value that the exchange price really amounts to deception. If this is done, it calls for unusual tactics of support that degenerate into rigging or pool tactics. Ordinary open and aboveboard tactics are insufficient.

[6] Oscar Lasdon, "Market Action of New Issues," *Commercial and Financial Chronicle*, Sept. 28, 1940, p. 1774.

Stabilization operations are sufficiently safeguarded by present regulations. Present rules governing the flotation of new issues and the operation of the stock exchanges control rigging, pool, and other manipulative activities. It is believed that under these rules there is no serious danger of abuses resulting from stabilization operations.

IV. SHOULD THE SEVERAL INVESTMENT BANKING FUNCTIONS BE SEGREGATED?

As shown in Chapter III, the business of investment banking includes three distinct types of operations or functions: (1) origination; (2) underwriting and purchasing; and (3) distribution to investors. Most investment banks, it was pointed out, engage at one time or another in all three types of operations. The performance of the underwriting function was frequently carried out jointly by a group of collaborating houses, including insurance companies and even individuals. This function, properly speaking, was simply the assumption of the risk that the securities might not all be marketed by the date agreed upon. For this service a special risk assumption or underwriting fee was given. When the issue was marketed the underwriting group was automatically dissolved.

In recent years government agencies have urged the segregation of underwriting and purchasing from distribution. Those believing in segregation maintain that the underwriter should concentrate on risk assumption and not be involved in the quite different task of finding retail markets for securities; and, in turn, that the dealer should be independent from the underwriter, thereby being in a position to give impartial advice to his investing clients. But as against this point of view, some contend that there is a positive advantage to the investor when the dealer has participated in the underwriting of a security which he also distributes, for he then has an implied responsibility for and professional pride in the quality of the issue.

A clear-cut segregation of operations appears undesirable. First, it would increase the costs of distribution, since each institution in the chain would have to make a separate investigation of the merits of the issue. Second, it would be especially to the disadvantage of the smaller investment banks which serve the needs of local business enterprises. In many parts of the country small, local, inactive issues must be both underwritten and sold by the same banking institution. This combination of operations is made necessary by the fact that, in many localities, underwriting capital comes only from a local institution which acts as an occasional underwriter. Morever, a local security can only be distributed by a selling organization which has previously underwritten and which therefore knows the details of the issue. There is no doubt that the separation of the two operations would seriously interefere with the distribution of the securities of small businesses.

In recent years the local dealer has become a more important factor in the distribution of securities. As pointed out by the president of the Investment Bankers Association "there has been a great change in the whole system of distributing securities. While in 1929 the bulk of the securities throughout the country was handled by branches of out-of-town houses, the lion's share of the business today is done by strictly local houses." [7] In view of the present importance of the local dealer, legislation segregating his operations would seriously interfere with the system of security distribution.

Underwriting, in the strict sense of carrying the risks of distribution, has lost much of its former significance so far as the larger issues are concerned. As noted on pages 26-28, underwriting developed to meet the needs of a situation in which the supply of investment money was usually meagre and the time required to place the securities in the hands of ultimate investors protracted and uncertain. But where the supply of investment funds is redundant as at present, the distribution of high-grade issues is a very quick process with the risks accordingly of negligible proportions. Under these circumstances, the charges that could legitimately be made for a pure underwriting service could hardly justify the maintenance of special institutions to perform this service.

Segregation of investment banking functions is impractical. Under present conditions segregation would be uneconomical even in the case of large issues. In the case of small issues, it would constitute a serious impediment. This would be especially true with issues handled by local houses in the smaller cities.

Another phase of the segregation issue relates to trading in securities already outstanding. In the past, members of stock exchanges have been permitted to act both as brokers and dealers in securities. The combined broker-dealer system has been an integral part of the security mechanism in the United States

---

[7] *Commercial and Financial Chronicle,* Nov. 11, 1943, p. 1879.

for over half a century. At the present time about a third of the active brokers registered with the Securities and Exchange Commission are also active dealers. The Securities and Exchange Act of 1934 authorized the Commission to make a study of the feasibility of segregating the broker-dealer function.

The performance of these two functions by the same party has been sharply criticized. It is pointed out that one and the same person acts in the capacity of broker as *agent* of his client and in the capacity of dealer as *principal* in his own behalf in the buying and selling of securities. It is urged that one class of persons should act as brokers or agents for their customers, and a distinctly separate class should serve as dealers or principals in security transactions. This segregation would apply to the exchanges and to over-the-counter markets as well.

Those favoring the segregation of the broker-dealer function point to the practice of the London Stock Exchange. It is claimed that on this market the membership is divided between brokers who handle customers' orders and dealers or jobbers who execute transactions for their own account. It should, however, be noted that in actual practice the separation of these functions is not complete. Moreover, the transactions on the London market are not conducted in the full light of publicity. There is no ticker system which discloses individual transactions and price changes as in the United States. If he wishes, the London broker or dealer merely turns in slips recording the transactions and prices.

The exchanges have imposed careful restrictions on the trading operations of specialists. For example, the New York Stock Exchange rule 365 provides that:

No specialist shall effect on the exchange purchases or sales of any security in which such specialist is registered, for any account in which he or his firm, or any partner thereof, is directly or indirectly interested, unless such dealings are reasonably necessary to permit such specialist to maintain a fair and orderly market, or to act as an odd-lot dealer in such security.

It is also required that in any transaction where a specialist combines the broker-dealer function in a single transaction, it must immediately be reported to the broker for whom the specialist was acting.

Brokerage and dealing operations should not be segregated. The existing combination broker-dealer system has not been characterized by abuses. Existing rules and close supervision by both the Stock Exchanges and the Securities and Exchange Commission provide ample safeguards.

V. IS PRIVATE PLACEMENT DESIRABLE?

A striking development of the thirties was the rise of so-called *private placement,* whereby capital funds are raised directly without the aid of an intermediary investment bank. It assumes two forms: (1) the direct placement of an issue with insurance companies or other investing institutions; these issues are commonly in the form of bonds or preferred stock, since such institutions are not permitted to invest in common stock; and (2) the "term loan" which is obtained from commercial banks. Such loans commonly run from five to ten years and are payable serially.

A combination of factors is responsible for this bypassing of the investment banker. On the one hand, it avoids the expenses, delays, disclosure requirements, and potential civil liabilities involved with issues subject to S.E.C. regulations. A privately placed issue is also free from the restrictions of other legislation such as the Trust Indenture Act of 1939. The significance of this evasion factor is indicated by the fact that private placement has developed mainly in those classes of securities which are subject to S.E.C. control. Public utility and industrial issues, which are subject to S.E.C. regulation, account for 96 per cent of the total, while railroad issues, which fall outside S.E.C. jurisdiction, account for only 4 per cent.[8]

Another important factor in the development of both direct placement and the term loan is the abundance of investment money in recent years as compared with the supply of new issues. Both the insurance companies and the commercial banks have been hard put to find investment outlets—other than in low-yield government bonds. If limited to participation in issues distributed through regular channels, an institution may get but a small fraction of any issue; whereas by direct negotiation it may obtain an entire issue. A very large issue or loan may be split among a group of co-operating institutions. Competition for investments on the part of investing institutions has perhaps been of equal importance with the desire of issuing corporations to avoid the regulations of the S.E.C. or to obtain more flexible terms than are possible with public offerings.

The term loan has also been unwittingly encouraged by some of the regulations of the Comptroller of

[8] *Proposed Amendments to the Securities Act of 1933 and to the Securities Exchange Act of 1934,* Hearings before the House Committee on Interstate and Foreign Commerce, 77 Cong. 1 sess., Pt. 2, p. 373. See detailed table.

the Currency pertaining to bank investments. A regulation of June 27, 1938 prohibits national banks and state member banks from purchasing "investment securities" in which the "investment characteristics are distinctly or predominantly speculative." This ruling applies to "investments" but not to "loans." It is therefore possible for banks to purchase corporate obligations as loans when they could not be acquired as public offerings. For example, a group of banks purchased from the International Telephone and Telegraph Company its 4.5 per cent notes, although this company's outstanding debentures would not have been eligible under the regulations.

Privately placed securities have been sold mainly to large institutional investors. This is revealed in a study of such securities over a seven-year period from 1934 through 1940. This study traced the purchasers of 77 per cent of all the private issues placed over these years. Of these issues, about 92 per cent went to 20 purchasers; about 60 per cent were sold to three large institutional buyers, and one company accounted for over 25 per cent.[9]

To the institutional buyer private placement has decided advantages. Large security purchasers have been able to place their funds in corporate obligations without coming under the provisions of the securities legislation.

To the general public, private placement has brought distinct disadvantages. The individual and the small institutional investors have been faced with a growing inability to place their funds in high-grade corporate obligations, since they have been mainly purchased privately by large institutional investors.

[9] The same, p. 370. See detailed table.

The volume of securities available for the free open market has necessarily declined under private placement, since the institutional investors do not generally resell their holdings. In general, it may be said that the method of private placement has operated only to the advantage of the large institutional investor.

Direct placement of both types (placement with institutions and term loans) is opposed by investment bankers on several grounds. First, they regard it as an unwarranted taking over of their function. This is especially the case where insurance companies resell securities acquired without registration. For example, it was reported that the Equitable Life Assurance Company sold the debentures of the Socony Vacuum Oil Company which had been purchased at private sale.[10] In another case the Equitable bought a $35,000,000 issue of utility bonds, and four months later resold $10,000,000 of these bonds to twenty other insurance companies.[11] In these transactions the insurance company was really acting in the capacity of a distributor, without assuming the liabilities imposed by the S.E.C. on security distributors. If fully developed, this practice might eventually emasculate security regulation.

Second, the investment bankers contend that this practice results in depriving the investing public of a chance to purchase the cream of new security offerings. They have to be content with what is left after the insurance companies and banks have taken what they want, which usually means inferior securities that do not qualify as legal investments. In periods when the volume of new issues is relatively small,

[10] The same, Pt. 2, p. 386.
[11] The same, Pt. 3, p. 689.

this factor in the situation may be of vital concern to individual investors, administrators of trust funds, educational institutions, and the smaller savings institutions.

Third, it is feared that the loss by the investment bankers of this substantial part of their normal business may so weaken the investment banking machinery that it will be unable to render the services required by the investing public in connection with the underwriting and distributing of lesser issues. The outcome might be either the drying up of the security distribution business or increasing charges in order to live. The result in either case would be unfortunate from the point of view of raising capital for enterprises which have not reached the stage of assured earnings and high stability.

Direct placement should be permitted but be subject to the same regulations as public offerings. It should not be prohibited because it may be an economical means of raising funds. Section 4-1 of the Securities Act should be amended to include a definition of security offerings broad enough to cover privately placed issues. This would even the plane of competition between investment bankers, on the one hand, and insurance companies and commercial banks on the other.

VI. SHOULD THE INVESTMENT BANKING SYSTEM BE DECENTRALIZED?

In all countries, the evolution of investment banking and security dealings was in the direction of concentration in a few great financial centers. In each country a single market came to occupy a position of dominant importance—New York, London, Amsterdam, Paris, Berlin, Tokyo, etc. This trend was a natural accompaniment of the growth in the size of the business unit, necessitated by large accumulations of capital. Local markets existed in the early years of the evolution of the investment banking system, but they gradually became less important. Manchester in England, Lyons in France, Frankfort in Germany, and Philadelphia in the United States are illustrations of markets which gradually declined in importance.

In the great financial centers a few institutions came to occupy positions of dominant importance. In many cases they conducted both commercial and investment operations. In some cases, also, notably in Germany and Japan, these financial institutions were intimately associated with vast business enterprises. The degree of concentration was on the whole greater in other countries than in the United States—a reflection no doubt of the vast area and great diversity of economic life found in the United States.

In the United States the great concentration of financial power, especially in the field of investment banking, has long been regarded with concern. This was reflected in the well-known insurance and money trust investigations in the period 1910-14. The financial collapse of 1929-33, as indicated in an earlier chapter, intensified the opposition to financial concentration and the interlocking relationships between commercial and investment banking institutions. As already noted, this led to the segregation of investment and commercial institutions. At the same time, the power hitherto exercised by the Federal Reserve Bank of New York was transferred to the Federal Reserve Board in Washington.

In the light of these trends it was not surprising

that many should also have expressed themselves strongly in favor of a thoroughgoing decentralization of the investment banking and security business. William O. Douglas, when chairman of the Commission, summarized the case as follows:

The development of regional financing should bring with it these conditions. First and foremost it should bring simpler and more conservative finance where finance is brought closer to the locus of business and where investors are brought closer to finance and investment.

Second, regional financing should produce better-planned financing, since under that system there might be greater freedom from the scramble in the central capital market for the issues of temporarily popular industries.

Third, regional finance might be able to develop an adequate organization for the supply of long-term capital, particularly in equity form, to enterprises of moderate size.

Fourth, a reduction in absentee financing would result in a reduction of absentee ownership and management, with all the advantages which flow from keeping business at home for the home folks.

Finally, the development of regional capital markets would bring new capital and new brains into the investment banking industry and the financial management of local business. Regional capital markets of sufficient stature should help retain and employ the best of their own sons at home.[12]

While the goals thus set forth have not been realized in ensuing years, it is true, as indicated in the preceding section, that security distribution by local houses has become much more important relatively speaking than was formerly the case. This is due in large part to the decline in fund raising by large corporations, for reasons indicated in Chapter I. Meanwhile, there was no corresponding decline in the financial requirements of smaller enterprises; and the opportunity thus

[12] William O. Douglas, *Democracy and Finance,* p. 31.

remained for alert investment houses to serve the needs of such a clientele.

The financing of the medium- and smaller-sized local industries is carried out in part by local investment houses, and in part also by houses which operate on a nation-wide scale. The local house in the main provides a local market for the securities. The larger national organization, by virtue of its many branches, is able to provide a broader market. Moreover, it makes available to local enterprises the knowledge and experience gained through a broadly diversified business.

Decentralization of the investment banking system is unnecessary. In view of (1) the set-up and character of American business enterprise, (2) the abundance of funds which are now available for investment purposes, and (3) the adaptations which investment banking has made to accommodate the needs of medium- and small-sized businesses, we see no reason at present for attempting to force greater decentralization.

VII. HOW CAN SECURITY LEGISLATION BE SIMPLIFIED?

Over the years an enormous mass of federal and state legislation has accumulated. In order to simplify this vast legislative maze the following recommendations are made:

Federal security legislation should be integrated. In order to eliminate confusion and duplication, the Securities Act, the Securities Exchange Act, the Trust Indenture Act, the provisions of the Public Utility Holding Company Act, the Investment Company Act, and the Bankruptcy Act should be re-drafted into a single code.

Federal and state securities legislation should be co-ordinated. The lack of co-ordination between federal and state security legislation complicates the flotation of issues. It is sometimes necessary to qualify a new issue of stock several times. Thus, the stock of a company may have to be registered under the federal act and also registered or qualified under several state laws before it can be sold. At times as many as six different documents must be prepared.[13] This problem is particularly aggravated if the underwriters wish to effect a wide distribution of an issue. As a result, the cost in paper work and legal fees is greatly increased.

It has been recommended that securities registered under the federal securities act be automatically exempt from all state securities laws. This proposal has been criticized in that it would extend the powers of the S.E.C.

Each state should rather adopt a brief amendment to its security law that its requirements would be met by filing a copy of the registration statement under the S.E.C. provided this statement includes any additional data required by the state law.

Seasoned issues should be exempt from the registration requirement. A distinction should be drawn between the registration of seasoned and unseasoned issues. The Securities Act at present makes no such distinction, and its provisions are applied with equal force against both classes of securities.

[13] John W. Kearns, "Coordination of Securities Acts" 31 *Illinois Law Review* 719 (1937).

The original draft of the Securities Act exempted from its provisions not only railroad but also public utility securities.[14] However, at that time state regulation of utilities was not uniform or even complete, and the proposal for the exemption of public utilities was therefore dropped. In recent years there has been a marked improvement in state utility legislation. The Public Utility Holding Company Act confers upon the Commission broad powers in the financing of utilities in general. The laws of most leading states exempt from registration the securities of public utility corporations regulated by state and federal commissions, securities listed on recognized stock exchanges, and legal investments.[15] A similar exemption might well be adopted by the federal government.

VIII. HOW CAN THE REGISTRATION PROCEDURE BE IMPROVED?

The changes suggested below would, it is believed, go far toward eliminating the difficulties which have arisen in the past.

The registration statement should be simplified and made definite. The statement should consist of a general prospectus conforming to certain definite standards set by the Commission.[16] A special committee on security laws and regulations of the American Bar Association holds that if this proposal were accepted "there would be small likelihood of any real increase in risk to investors, while the hindrances to the flotation of new issues would be appreciably

---

[14] *Proposed Amendments to the Securities Act of 1933 and to the Securities Exchange Act of 1934,* House Hearings, Pt. 3, p. 756.

[15] For summary of these laws see the same, Pt. 1, p. 200.

[16] The same, Pt. 3, p. 711.

eased." [17] The report criticizes the present registration statement and prospectus requirements in the following words: "The trouble and expense of preparing a Securities Act registration statement and prospectus has been one of the major difficulties with the act, while the development of the prospectus into a document far too complex and unwieldy for its purpose has been one of the act's major failures." [18] Chairman Purcell of the Commission has testified that "the Commission is in agreement with the industry on certain proposals designed to get into the hands of the prospective purchasers a simplified form of prospectus not loaded with a lot of detail, which he can read with ease and make up his mind what he can do about it." [19]

Duplication in registration statements should be eliminated. At present a company may be required to file registration statements several times. Thus the company may be called upon to submit statements not only under the Securities Act but also under the Investment Company Act. A public utility may in addition be required to file statements under the Public Utility Holding Company Act.

A company which has already filed registration statements under any of the security acts should be required to file an additional registration statement consisting merely of the general prospectus and any other information which the Commission may deem necessary.

The prospectus should be simplified. Mr. Ganson Purcell, chairman of the Commission, has admitted

---

[17] The same, Pt. 1, p. 165.
[18] The same, Pt. 3, p. 710.
[19] The same, Pt. 1, p. 34.

that "probably the prospectus is not serving completely the purpose for which it was designed . . . It is not being read from cover to cover by as many of the investors as the Congress would have liked." [20] The Commission favors the proposal of the simplified prospectus.

IX. WHAT CHANGES SHOULD BE MADE IN THE WAITING PERIOD?

The speed of security distribution has often been criticized. The congressional report which introduced the original Securities Act singled out this feature of the investment banking mechanism for particularly bitter attack.[21]   This critical attitude towards speed in security distribution influenced the drafting of the act. The chairman of the S.E.C., in reviewing the passage of the act, said that this characteristic "gave grave concern to the Congress." [22] He added:

Prior to the Securities Act the underwriter would sell a large part of each new issue to subunderwriters and to the selling group dealers substantially simultaneously with his original purchase of the securities from the issuer. This, of course, resulted in the immediate elimination of a great part of the risk which otherwise would fall on the originating underwriter. However, the underwriting compensation to the originating underwriter was paid regardless of how much had been taken up by or sold to the selling group members at just about the same time as the underwriter's original purchase of the issue.[23]

As a result of this hostile attitude towards speed much effort has been made by the government to slow up security distribution.

[20] The same, Pt. 1, p. 33.
[21] H. Rept. 85, 73 Cong. 1 sess., p. 6.
[22] *Proposed Amendments to the Securities Act of 1933 and to the Securities Exchange Act of 1934,* House Hearings, Pt. 1, p. 9.
[23] The same.

The waiting period, as described in Chapter III, has been the leading device used to attain this objective. In 1940 the Securities Act was amended to speed up the waiting period. The so-called "acceleration of the effective date" permits the Commission to make the registration of any issue effective at a date earlier than the twentieth day. (Amendment to section 8 [a]). The Commission has followed a liberal policy in administering this new section. In fact it has permitted registration statements to become effective as quickly as six or seven days after filing.[24] Under these conditions there is little need of a further shortening of the waiting period. Investment bankers naturally favor a further reduction of the waiting period, but it is difficult to see how this could be accomplished without destroying the basic principles of the Securities Act.

The provisions of the Securities Act regarding solicitations during the waiting period should be modified. The act very properly encourages a banker to circulate information regarding a forthcoming issue but at the same time forbids him to make any "attempt to offer to dispose of an issue." [25] Violations of this section subject the banker to criminal liability and to possible revocation of his over-the-counter dealer license.[26] It is necessary to remove the inconsistency of an encouragement to give information during the waiting period and at the same time an imposition of penalties for making or soliciting offers. Oral offers and solicitations should be permitted

[24] *Report of the Securities and Exchange Commission on Proposals for Amendments to the Securities Act,* House Committee on Interstate and Foreign Commerce, 77 Cong. 1 sess., p. 5.

[25] Secs. 20, 24.

[26] Sec. 15-d.

before the effective date. The actual sale of securities should still be prohibited. It should also be required that the prospective purchaser receive the prospectus within a reasonable time before he agrees to purchase the issue.[27]

X. WHAT SHOULD BE THE LIABILITY UNDER SECURITIES LEGISLATION?

There has been a strong public demand that directors should be fully charged with the responsibility of their office. As stated in the congressional report urging the passage of the Securities Act: "directors should assume the responsibility of directing and if their manifold activities make real directing impossible, they should be held responsible to the unsuspecting public for their neglect." [28]

The liability provisions under the Securities Act are, however, very sweeping. The statute provides that the purchaser of a security registered under the act may seek and obtain damages for losses if the registration statement contains any misstatement of a material fact or omits any such statement. These damages may be obtained not only from the corporation but also from its officers, directors, accountants, experts, and underwriters. The burden of proof rests upon the defendant. These provisions also apply to misstatements in the reports of the company required under the act. A director may be held liable even if he did not sign the registration statement or even know of its existence.[29]

---

[27] For discussion see, *Report of Securities and Exchange Commission on Proposals for Amendments*, p. 9.

[28] William O. Douglas, "Directors Who Do Not Direct," 47 *Harvard Law Review* 1305.

[29] Sec. 2. For discussion see 49 *Yale Law Review* 1432.

It would seem reasonable that a party should have the right to set up, as a defense against his liability, the proof that he did not know or did not have a reasonable basis for believing the facts stated to be untrue.

A single standard of civil liability should be formulated. At present there is a wide divergence in these liabilities under the several securities statutes. This is evidenced from a reading of sections 11 and 12 of the Securities Act and section 18 of the Securities Exchange Act. Such a single standard would eliminate the present and confusing details on this important subject.

INDEX